Your Kids and Divorce

Other books by Thomas A. Whiteman

With Bob Burns
    The Fresh Start Divorce Recovery Workbook
With Michele Novotni
    Adult ADD
With Randy Petersen
    Stress Test
    Be Your Own Best Friend
    Starting Over

Your Kids and Divorce

Helping Them Grow beyond the Hurt

Thomas A. Whiteman, Ph.D.

Fleming H. Revell
A Division of Baker Book House Co
Grand Rapids, Michigan 49516

© 1992, 2001 by Thomas A. Whiteman

Published by Fleming H. Revell
a division of Baker Book House Company
P.O. Box 6287, Grand Rapids, MI 49516-6287

Updated edition. Previously published as *Innocent Victims: Understanding the Needs and Fears of Your Children* by Thomas Nelson, 1992.

Printed in the United States of America

Library of Congress Cataloging-in-Publication Data

Whiteman, Tom.
    Your kids and divorce : helping them grow beyond the hurt / Thomas
A. Whiteman.
        p.   cm.
    Includes bibliographical references.
    ISBN 0-8007-5775-0
    1. Children of divorced parents—Psychology. 2. Children of divorced parents—Family relationships. 3. Children of divorced parents—Life skills guides. I. Title.
HQ777.5 .W534 2001
306.874—dc21   2001041737

The quote from Charles Swindoll on pages 196 and 197 is taken from *Strengthening Your Grip* (Nashville: Word, Inc., 1982) and is used by permission. All rights reserved.

For current information about all releases from Baker Book House, visit our web site:
http://www.bakerbooks.com

Contents

Introduction

Divorce hurts. I have talked with thousands of men and women who have gone through divorce, and I've perceived their deep wounds. My message to them is consistently this: You can recover. No matter how deeply pained you are right now, things will get better. You can grow out of this bad experience.

The same is true for children of divorce. Often they suffer more than their parents do. Their lives are torn apart and they're not sure why. They're flooded with emotions they don't understand. Sometimes they blame themselves for the upheaval. No doubt about it. It's tough to be a kid when your parents split up. But my message to them is the same: You can recover. No matter how deeply pained you are right now, things will get better. You can grow out of this bad experience.

Bad Press

Author Judith Wallerstein recently came out with a book about the effects of divorce on children, *The Unexpected Legacy of Divorce* (Hyperion, 2000). She has done some intriguing work, tracing the paths of a group of children whose parents divorced in the 1970s. Now those children are well into adulthood. Wallerstein documents the tragic effects of divorce in their lives. As a group, they are insecure, unfulfilled, and unable to sustain good relationships. Her conclusion: Divorce destroys kids. A lousy marriage is still better than a good divorce. Parents should stay together for the sake of their kids.

This latest book has generated a lot of press, including a *Time* cover story. Suddenly people are warning that divorce does irreparable harm to children. I've been asked what I think of Wallerstein's work. Well, I can't argue with her main conclusion, namely, that divorce is bad and parents should stay together. I firmly believe in marriage. Husbands and wives should stay together not only for the children but also to remain true to their marriage vows.

But I deal every day with people who have already made the divorce choice. They have divorced, and now they're picking up the pieces. Is there any hope for them? Judith Wallerstein makes a strong case for despair. She shows us a group of divorce victims, children whose lives were broken by their broken homes. If she's trying to scare parents into staying married, fine. But her analysis isn't very helpful for those who have already divorced, or for their children.

As research goes, Wallerstein's work is deep but not wide. She gives detailed portraits of a small group of people. Other research has examined larger groups and found that the outlook isn't quite so bleak. These other studies, more statistically significant, show that many children of divorce rise above their circumstances. They learn to have good relationships. They become happy adults.

Time quotes Robert Emery, director of the University of Virginia's Center for Children, Families, and the Law: "I think [Wallerstein] is wonderful at seeing the trees, but sometimes she misses the forest. For the most part, kids from divorced families are resilient. They bounce back from all the stresses. Some kids are at risk, but the majority are functioning well" (*Time*, September 25, 2000, p. 77).

There *is* hope. Children of divorce are not doomed to lead second-rate lives. You can help them get through this crisis. You can help them become stronger through it. The children Wallerstein studied came from the first big wave of divorce in the 1970s. Maybe that explains why they had such difficulty—it was all so new, no one knew how to help them cope. But over the years, we have reached greater understanding of the effects of divorce on everyone involved. Books like this one have helped children put their lives back together.

In its first printing, this book was called *Innocent Victims*. I called it that because it always seemed that, as moms and dads were struggling with dismantling their marriages, the innocent kids were suffering because of their parents' decisions. But since then I've realized that these children don't have to be victims. They can face the hard times with tremendous resiliency and emerge as victors. That is my message, my hope, and my prayer for the children of all those reading this book.

An Overview

This book is divided into three sections. Part 1 (chapters 1 and 2) is designed to help you understand how children of divorce are different from adults who are going through divorce. The focus of the second part (chapters 3–7) is how children of divorce are different from children of intact families. I explore both short-term and long-term reactions to the divorce experience. Part 3 (chapters 8–10) provides specific guidelines as to how you can minimize these differences and help your children recover by developing a new and healthy lifestyle.

The appendix at the end of the book provides a list of additional resources for further reading on specific issues dealt with in this book.

Where I'm Coming From

This book has grown out of an obvious need. The need has been dramatically felt by all those who have watched their children react to the disruption of their family. This was specifically brought to my attention quite vividly through my involvement with the Fresh Start Seminars.

Fresh Start Seminars began as a program for separated and divorced adults to help them grow beyond their pain to a point of acceptance in an entirely new lifestyle. The leadership team soon learned that one cannot effectively address the needs of the separated and divorced without helping them with their children. When we asked these "single again" folks what issues concerned them most, the first thing they listed was always the emotional survival of their children. Yet as I listened to their stories, I became aware that many well-educated adults seemed to be making major mistakes when it came to the needs of their children. I am writing this book in the hope of reaching as many of these parents as possible.

Yes, the statistics for children of divorce are discouraging. Yet I believe that early intervention can make an enormous difference in how well they do. Timely information and support for both children and parents can lessen the negative effects of divorce.

In 1982, at the outset of the Fresh Start divorce recovery program, parents by the dozens asked me: "When are you going to do something for our children?" I could hear their emotional cry for help, yet I felt ill-prepared to do anything. I remember thinking that someone should sponsor a program for these children. As I observed, listened, and read the research on the effects of divorce on children, the burden began to touch me more and more.

Having worked in the Philadelphia school district for six years as a school psychologist, I was very aware of the needs of divorced kids. About 80 percent of the students referred to me for emotional or educational problems came from single-parent families. To address this need within the school system, I started some small-group counseling sessions, specifically designed for the children of divorce. Through these few groups, I discovered just how necessary it was for these students to learn that there were other kids who were faced with similar difficulties, who were dealing with insecurity, emotional pain, and the embarrassment of coming from a family where Dad wasn't around or Mom just didn't care. The opportunity to talk about their experiences and to encourage one another proved to be very therapeutic for them and provided me with early insights into the needs of such children. In retrospect, I can see how I was being prepared for a ministry to children of divorce that would grow far beyond the Philadelphia area.

My next attempt to offer a program for children of divorce was during the Sunday school hour at my church.

I felt that the church was the ideal place for such a program because: (1) it typically addresses the needs of the traditional family at the exclusion of others, (2) the church includes the potential for whole family participation, and (3) the church should be a place of hope and healing, particularly for those who are struggling with difficult life issues.

The first week, only eight students attended the class. I knew many kids were embarrassed to come, feeling as if they were the only ones who did not fit into the Christian family stereotype. Some of these children had no father at home. Others had a mother who had abandoned the family. Somehow it did not seem "spiritual" to admit to such problems at home. Eventually, however, the students began to open up and trust one another. They became a significant support group and were a tremendous encouragement to me and to each other.

This class for the young victims of divorce grew in number. As it did, the students began to talk about other kids in their community who had no safe place to talk openly about what they were experiencing. They asked, "Why don't we do something for these other children of divorce?" This was the very question their parents had been asking me for years. The students pointed to the divorce recovery seminar offered by Fresh Start for adults and wondered why they couldn't have a similar seminar for kids. At this point all the pieces began to come together. So in 1987 we sponsored the first "Kids in the Middle" seminar at the Church of the Saviour, in Wayne, Pennsylvania. More than fifty children attended.

Today Fresh Start Seminars and Fresh Start for Kids are held in many locations throughout the United States and two foreign countries. We attempt to conduct the weekend seminars simultaneously so that whole families can come together for a time of insight and healing. Brochures and other materials are available through the Fresh Start office at:

Fresh Start Seminars
1440 Russell Rd.
Paoli, PA 19301
1-800-882-2799
e-mail: whitemant@aol.com
web site: www.freshstartseminars.org

This book is a direct outgrowth of that first seminar and the others that followed. It is designed to provide single parents and other concerned individuals with useful suggestions and new insights to help children who are experiencing the breakup of their family. With support and guidance, you can make a difference in the lives of these children.

Sometimes you won't want the information this book gives you. I won't gloss over the problems that divorce causes, but I want to emphasize again that there is hope. I wish that each of you could meet some of the children and teenagers that I interviewed in preparation for this book. Some had recently experienced their parental breakup, while others had been in single-parent or blended families for years. What I found in them I will not forget. They are some of the most loving, responsible, and sensitive kids I have ever met. It is easier to keep all the negative statistics in the proper perspective when you can sit down and talk with one of these young people face-to-face.

Part 1

Understanding Your Child

one

Through the Eyes of a Child

I will never forget Eddie Hyser. I was in fourth grade in a typical suburban classroom. It seemed as though each of the girls had long blond hair. Each of the boys had straight brown bangs hanging over his eyes. We all waited anxiously for lunch or recess . . . or summer! It must have been a simpler time because I don't ever remember hearing about child abuse, child pornography, or even custody battles. Each child came from the typical American home with two parents, a station wagon, and a safe neighborhood to play in. That is . . . except for Eddie.

Eddie was different. We all knew that Eddie came from a single-parent home. Whenever there was a problem in class, whenever something went wrong, or whenever there was a fight in the playground, we knew that somehow Eddie was involved. We liked Eddie well enough, but it seemed that, one by one, each of us would get in trouble when we played with Eddie. So one by one we either drew away from him or were forbidden by our parents to play with him.

I remember the time I got in trouble playing with Eddie and a couple of other boys. Someone was fooling with matches and somehow a fire got started. The fire burned a small field and the back of a garage. The police came and of course Eddie received primary blame. I got into trouble as well, but what I remember most was being told that I shouldn't play with Eddie. He was a "bad influence."

Eddie was the only classmate I can remember who came from a single-parent family. That seems strange to say in these days of widespread divorce, and I know that even then there must have been more families like Eddie's, yet I was completely unaware of their existence.

Of course that was a very different era. Not only was divorce rare, but when a divorce took place, there was much more of a stigma than there is today. Broken marriages were a hush-hush matter. We all sort of knew that Eddie didn't have a dad living with him, but no one talked about it. I think teachers and school principals gave Eddie a bit more leeway, too: "Of course he's a troubled kid. Look at the home he comes from!" But no one really understood what exactly his problems were or how to help him. Divorce was an unusual circumstance in that day and age, and we didn't know much about it.

Times have changed. Divorce rates are nudging 50 percent. About one million children go through the experience of a family breakup each year. And about one third of all American children will spend some time in a single-parent family before they reach the age of eighteen. Growing up in a divorced home is not a rare occurrence but rather a norm for today's society. In fact, with single parents, blended families, and unmarried parents, today it's kind of rare to find a kid with two parents still married to each other!

Divorce may seem more normal these days, but still it takes its toll on children. A generation ago we had one or two "Eddies" suffering through their parents' breakup. Now we have classrooms full of them. The same things that made Eddie a "troubled child" continue to trouble children in today's world. The trauma is just as real as ever, even though it's more common.

There's a bit of a silver lining, however. The prevalence of the problem has brought more attention to it in the last two decades. Psychologists and educators have studied the effects of divorce on children, and we now know more than we used to. For one thing, we no longer call these families "broken homes." That carries a negative connotation and implies failure. No, these are now "single-parent families." That change in terminology reflects the concept that the people involved in a divorce might be hurt, but they're not broken beyond repair. We are now more aware of how to help them.

This, by the way, is one factor that's often overlooked by researchers who study the long-term effects of divorce on children. Granted, many children whose parents divorced in the 1970s have grown up into relationship-challenged adults. They seem to be permanently handicapped by their parents' divorce. But the divorce boom was just starting back then. These kids were Eddies, who suffered not only from the divorce but also from the unusualness of it. They were no doubt branded as "troubled kids" from "broken homes," and their teachers and parents probably weren't sure what to do to help them.

Now we know more. The situation isn't hopeless, as some researchers imply. There are specific strategies that can help your children make the best of these bad circumstances.

Finding Serenity

But what if it's too late? What if you can't employ these strategies? I've talked with many parents who hear my suggestions and respond with frustration. They worry that they have already scarred their kids for life, or that they will somehow botch any new child-rearing plans. Parents can torment themselves over many things that are completely out of their control. If you are to survive as a single parent, you need to adopt the attitude that I believe is best expressed in the Serenity Prayer, which has been popularized by the Alcoholics Anonymous program: "God, grant me the serenity to accept the things that I cannot change, the courage to change the things that I can, and the wisdom to know the difference."

Keep this prayer in mind as you read this book. There are changes you can make that will have a very positive impact on your children. But there are some circumstances that may be quite negative and are beyond your control. You must let go of these things, except as matters of prayer. The really difficult part, and that which requires the greatest wisdom, is knowing which things you need to change and which you should leave with God.

Perhaps a simple example would be helpful. A common problem for divorcing parents, yet an important factor, is the parents' attitude toward their children and toward each other. You *can* control your own attitude, but you can't control the other parent. Many parents expend a lot of energy trying to get the other parent to be more loving or responsible when the kids are with him or her. Yet this may only worsen the problem, since your ex-spouse usually resents your input, and you end up only frustrating yourself. The frustration toward your ex-spouse can't help but be evident to your kids, who now view you as too busy with your own problems to be accessible to them.

The alternative, the more helpful solution, is to pray for the other parent's relationship with the children, while you concentrate on loving your children as best you can. Hugs, listening, or companionship at sporting events or concerts are concrete expressions of support that many single parents overlook because they are too busy thinking about what the other parent should be doing differently, or perhaps how they wish *they* were supported.

Understanding Your Child

When we try to understand why children act and react the way they do in response to divorce, we must first understand the different ways adults and children think. Many people mistakenly think of children as miniature adults. The truth is that the way children think and act is very different from adults. To help children of divorce, we must take these differences seriously.

Many parents believe that they need only to love and nurture their children, and then everything will turn out okay. As important as these ingredients are, it is impossible to truly love and nurture someone you don't understand. It takes a special effort to see the divorce situation through the eyes of a child. This is emphasized by Dr. Stuart Berger in his book *Divorce without Victims* (Houghton Mifflin, 1990):

> It is absolutely essential for the parent to realize that until the child reaches young adulthood, his view of the world and the people around him is very different from the adult's. Even the teenager, who appears full grown in so many ways, is somewhat at the mercy of his continuing physical and emotional development. Your behavior toward your child, whatever his age, during the period of parental separation and divorce, must take into account his particular stage of development (p. 16).

There are a number of important concepts concerning the way children think that adults must understand if they are to help their children through the trauma of divorce. In the next chapter we will look at a few of these key concepts. We will examine the ways in which the mind of the child differs from the mind of the adult.

All Alone

Even as prevalent as divorce has become, children still tend to feel as if they are the only ones going through such trauma. If, as an adult, you've gone through divorce, you know how lonely that experience is. Children feel the same way. Why? Well, there are several reasons.

First, most people, and especially children, don't think about the problem of divorce until it affects them directly. So while they may have met other children of divorce, it didn't make an impression on them. Even if they have close friends from single-parent families, they probably haven't considered the pain those friends must have felt in the breakup.

Second, children tend to be very egocentric, which means they pay attention only to themselves and the things that directly affect them. When they feel emotional pain, that's all they can focus on. In that moment, they have little awareness of the pain of others.

The third reason children feel that they are the only ones going through such difficulties is that most kids (and people in general) tend to keep to themselves the emotional hurts and trauma of a family breakup. The stigma of failure associated with divorce is less intense than it used to be, but it's still there. All members of a divorcing family tend to feel some shame about the experience and, therefore, they do not talk about what they are going through. Most children are taught to keep family matters private, so they do not talk in school about what's going on at home.

While working in the public school system, I was surprised to see how many students kept significant secrets from their classmates and teachers. Their elaborate schemes would include lying about weekend trips they had supposedly made with their "fantasy family" and making up wild stories about why both of their parents had not been able to attend a parent-teacher conference. However, their protection of the truth only thwarted opportunities that might have been available to them, such as support groups within the school. Or a classmate might have stepped forward to empathize with their experience—if only they were honest. But kids often guard the secret of divorce.

Summary

Attitudes toward divorce and children of divorce have changed, but there is still evidence of a significant stigma, perhaps one that the participants place on themselves, when families break up.

Children who experience the divorce of their parents tend to feel very alone and different, different from other children and different from their parents. Helping your child overcome these differences, and the negative emotions that go with them, is the topic of the third part of this book.

two

Why Don't We Think Alike?

Why don't our kids think the way we do? Many of us would respond that it's because we are older and wiser than our children. While this is probably true, this explanation doesn't do justice to the complex developmental differences between the child and the adult. In this chapter we will take a closer look at some of the key differences. These include the difference between the concrete thinking of the child and the abstract reasoning of the adult, between the egocentric thinking of the child and the adult's awareness of others, and between the magical thinking of the child and the adult's sense of reality.

Concrete Thinking

Kathy's parents separated when she was seven. When she spoke to me in counseling, she revealed that her father left the home because he and her mother had a fight. In reality Dad was involved with another woman and was planning a divorce so that he could marry his new lover. But Kathy thought her parents merely had a disagreement and would eventually make up. She went on to explain how she had squabbled with her best friend, and maybe they wouldn't speak to each other for a while, but they always worked things out.

Kathy said she knew her father was going to move back to their home very soon, because he had said that he still loved her very much. "Everyone knows that you don't leave someone you love," reasoned Kathy. "Both of my parents have always taught me that."

What Kathy concluded was a combination of what she had been told and what she had experienced firsthand. It's an example of the concrete thinking common to children. Adults have the capacity to think abstractly. This is our ability to go beyond the specific situation and to make conclusions that we have not been taught. For example, if Kathy were older (perhaps twelve or older, depending on her developmental maturity), she might conclude that even when people love each other, they don't always act in loving ways. Or she might figure out that people don't break off their marriages merely because of a fight and that there must be more going on than Dad is admitting.

Another example of a child's concrete thinking is found in the way children view morality. Children usually begin to view right and wrong according to whatever their parents teach them. They can't reason for themselves yet.

As they grow older, they begin to modify their parents' views according to their own experiences and input from teachers and friends. This new morality of theirs, however, is still merely a black-and-white view of what is right and wrong, based on the child's experiences. There is a general inability to deal with any gray areas, and therefore children tend to be very legalistic.

As children mature, so does their ability to reason abstractly. They begin to understand the intentions and motives of others. They become more flexible and understanding toward individual differences. Therefore they gain the ability to empathize with others even when they have never been through similar situations. Let me illustrate this development through some examples.

Why don't you steal? Your earliest memory as a child probably dictated that you shouldn't steal because your mommy or daddy said that it was bad. Perhaps later you observed other kids stealing toys and getting away with it. But just before you concluded that it was okay to steal, you saw someone get caught. So you learned that you shouldn't steal because you would be punished if you got caught. But by the time you reached adulthood, you probably began to realize many other reasons for not stealing, even if you knew there was no way you would get caught.

It is interesting to note that some adults never reach this final stage of reasoning. They go through life believing that it's okay to steal as long as you don't get caught. This is not only tragic, but it also indicates an immature or dysfunctional development of their moral reasoning.

Concrete thinking deals entirely with the here and now. It is generally not concerned with consequences or intentions, nor does it take into account the feelings of others.

Therefore, a child views divorce in terms of how it affects him now.

This plays into the egocentric thinking we'll be discussing next. "My family broke up because of me." "I'm the only one going through this." "What am I going to do now?" I have heard these statements from the children of divorce again and again. Many children will not understand that there are other kids going through the same trauma, until they see them and talk to them personally.

There is a transitional period somewhere between the years of twelve and twenty when teens gradually develop abstract reasoning skills. But divorce tends to delay this maturation process, since children will usually retreat to earlier stages of response when they feel threatened.

I remember Peter. He first came to see me as a ten-year-old fifth-grade student who was showing signs of emotional difficulties. His teacher referred him to me because he was very withdrawn and seemingly depressed. After hearing this description, I was surprised when, after the first few minutes of our meeting, Peter began to open up and pour out his emotional concerns. He described his parents' separation, which occurred when he was about five years old. He had many questions about it then but didn't know how to ask them. He didn't remember any explanation as to why his daddy left.

For five years Peter lived with these unanswered questions. Since explanation and counsel had not been given, he concluded that he must have been a pretty bad boy, so bad that he forced his father to leave. But he kept this conclusion to himself. Teachers and fellow students had no idea what was wrong because Peter never talked about it. He had become emotionally isolated.

Peter explained to me that he felt different because he was the only one in the school who had no father at home. When I heard this, I realized how emotionally isolated he was. This was a city school with more than 50 percent of its students coming from single-parent families! Still Peter had no idea that these other kids were struggling through the painful breakup of their homes, just as he was.

Peter's recovery was fairly rapid once we got to the heart of the problem and began to address the issues. I asked Peter to go home and ask his mom why she and his dad had broken up. In the meantime I called his mother and advised her to answer his questions as openly and honestly as she could, giving concrete examples as to why the marriage could not work. She was surprised by my request, since the breakup had happened five years earlier. In her mind it was all over and done with. But what was settled in her adult mind was far from settled in her son's.

I then started a counseling group in Peter's class for those who were from single-parent families. They openly shared their embarrassment of feeling all alone and different. But their very presence there provided concrete evidence of the fact that they were sharing the same experience. All of them, including Peter, needed to know that.

Before long, Peter began to feel more connected with his class. He no longer felt different or unusual. He began to speak up and interact with his classmates. He also learned from his mom that he was not to blame for his dad's leaving, and therefore he began to feel better about himself.

Divorcing parents should never assume that their kids will figure out on their own what went wrong. Children need very concrete explanations. This is one reason many kids have an especially difficult time accepting separation or divorce in cases where there has been little or no fighting by the parents—at least in front of them. I'm not suggesting that couples should *try* to fight in front of their children, but when there has been little concrete evidence of a problem, it's no wonder that kids have a hard time accepting the marital breakup. Children need explanations and concrete examples that they will be able to understand.

A child will generally relate the family breakup to whatever disruptive event happened most recently in the home. This is another example of concrete thinking. The younger the child, the greater the tendency to react in this way, since their memories are not well developed.

When Sally, a seven-year-old second-grader, brought home a bad report card, her parents yelled at her. This led to a big fight between Mom and Dad, which culminated in her father's storming out of the home. It was not surprising then that Sally informed me that her father left because *she* had gotten bad grades.

Then there's the six-year-old boy who informed me that his father left because Mommy made the wrong thing for dinner. You can imagine what happened in that home just before Daddy walked out the door.

As a parent, what can you do about your child's concrete thinking? Well, you cannot hurry a child's emotional or mental development. Like physical maturation, emotional development is generally predetermined and will only happen as a result of natural processes. However, divorce does tend to cause children to retreat in their development. This is not because their maturity process is naturally slower, but only because insecure kids will tend to do and think things that are familiar and comfortable to them. They are not willing to stretch themselves with new challenges when their world is falling apart.

Fortunately the developmental process balances out as children's lives begin to stabilize. As a parent, you need to try to provide as stable an environment as you can, as quickly as you can after the breakup of the family. Stability should be your number one priority, not finding another spouse.

Help your child by giving honest, clear information. Your child's questions deserve concrete answers, because this is the only kind of answer your child will understand. "Why did Daddy leave?" deserves "Because when Daddy and Mommy are together, we fight a lot and that makes us both very unhappy." Or, "Because Daddy loves someone else and wants to be with her." Or maybe, "I'm sorry but I just don't know why Daddy left." If that's the truth, then that's what your answer should be. But if you do tell your child you don't know why Daddy or Mommy left, you'd better discover an answer as soon as possible and let your child know the truth.

Egocentric Thinking

Kids are basically self-centered. Most people are aware of that fact, but did you know that it's a normal and necessary stage of development? This means that children go through a time when they believe that the whole world revolves around them. For example, very young children believe that the entire family has dinner at 5:30 P.M. because that's when *they* (the children) are hungry. Children are not capable of thinking any other way. And the younger the children, the more egocentric they are likely to be.

When my daughter was one year old, she believed the only reason that Mommy and Daddy existed was to satisfy her every desire. She whined when she wanted to eat and again when she was tired. If you try to tell a one- or two-year-old: "I'm sorry I can't pick you up right now; I'm busy," you probably won't get much sympathy.

Children retain some degree of egocentric thinking well into adolescence. They gradually change because of their increasing awareness of others and their growing ability to understand abstractly other people's points of view.

Let me share an example of how people's ability to think abstractly begins to change their egocentricity. Did you ever wonder why elementary and junior high kids can be so cruel to their classmates, particularly to those who are different or handicapped in some way? This is an example of egocentric *and* concrete thinking. "It doesn't hurt *me*." Children are generally unable to abstractly put themselves into other people's shoes and empathize with how they must feel. They don't understand or care how others feel, just how they feel about others. Therefore parents should not expect their children to empathize with them over their divorce. The child can feel only his own pain.

As a parent, you may try to explain over and over why picking on others is wrong. You may urge your children to look at things from someone else's point of view. Yet it seems as though you're wasting your breath. Then gradually, and strangely independent of your efforts, your children get to a certain age and begin to feel empathy or compassion for others who are suffering. (This often happens as they enter their teens, but sometimes earlier. Usually girls are about six months to a year ahead of the boys.) The teasing of the less fortunate dissipates to a point where many young adults will begin to really reach out to others less fortunate than themselves.

It is unfortunate but true that many teenagers and some adults continue to be thoroughly self-centered well beyond the age when they should know better. This is usually not a reflection of their *inability* to understand how others feel, but it may stem from bad habits, a family pattern, or a personality trait. The difference between the adult and child is that the child is not capable of thinking about the feelings of others and having compassion for them, while the adult is capable but may choose not to do it.

How does egocentric thinking relate to the divorce experience? Divorce tends to make this egocentric thinking become more pronounced and obvious. Even the most giving adults will retreat emotionally and begin to focus on self-protection when they go through a divorce. So imagine how children, who are naturally egocentric, tend to respond!

One teenager told me, "Here I am just getting to the point where I'm ready to start dating and my mom and dad pull this. How am I ever going to bring someone home to meet my parents when they're not even together?"

Another student said, "Now that this has happened, what are we going to do about my birthday party next year?"

Maybe you've never heard your child say anything like this, but they've probably thought it. And, considering the normal egocentrism of children—raised to a higher power by the trauma of divorce—it's not as cold as it sounds. Children are *supposed* to think of themselves first.

Egocentric thinking may also cause children and teenagers to become angry with the custodial parent. They expect their parent to do something about the separation or divorce. And they may be too self-centered to realize that their parent is powerless to change the circumstances. It doesn't seem right for a young mother, abandoned by her husband, to be blamed by her children for "making Daddy go away," but that can happen. Egocentric thinking in children of divorce can produce painful situations, but parents should remember that this is the child's nature, not a malicious behavior.

Another by-product of egocentric thinking is that children begin to greatly overestimate their own importance. Therefore they cannot imagine anything happening that they did not somehow cause. This presents one more reason why so many children of divorce, like Peter and Sally, believe they were somehow to blame for their parents' breakup. In the mind of the child, if everything revolves around them, then it is logical to assume that Mom or Dad left *because* of them.

Research indicates that more than half of all children and teens who experience the breakup of their families believe that they were at least partially to blame. This phenomenon is due, I believe, to a combination of two factors: concrete thinking and egocentrism.

For this reason it is extremely important that you constantly reassure your children that they had nothing to do with the breakup of the family. *Don't assume that they know this. Don't assume that they will ask if they have any questions.* Continue to reassure them as they grow and develop that they were not the cause of the breakup. They need to hear this over and over until they are mature enough to truly comprehend what they have been through.

Why should you bother to explain such complex matters to your children if they don't have the capacity to understand such things? Because someday they will.

Each night, as I put my children to bed, I tell them I love them. I've been doing this since their infancy. You probably do the same. Does a two-year-old know what that means? Does an infant understand the meaning of love?

As your child hears the information over and over, he gains a superficial understanding of what it means. And as children grow, the depth of the meaning of your words becomes increasingly clear, until one day your children finally realize the significance of what you have been telling them all along.

So it is with children's understanding of the issues surrounding their parents' divorce. Each new stage of development brings with it not only new understandings but new questions, which previously had not been considered.

Magical Thinking

As children, we always enjoyed a good nursery rhyme or a short children's tale. One reason we enjoyed them is because the characters always lived "happily ever after." This happily-ever-after thinking corresponds to the magical thinking common to children. Children believe that somehow everything is going to turn out okay because they wish it to be.

I recall the freckle-faced six-year-old boy in my office who told me he felt bad because he had wished his father were dead. I asked him why that made him feel bad. He responded that by wishing his father were dead, he was afraid that he would cause his dad to really die.

At the time I thought it unusual for this boy to believe that he could wish his father to death. Yet in terms of magical thinking it makes perfect sense. The boy believed he could bring it to pass by thinking it.

Dr. Stuart Berger in *Divorce without Victims* wrote:

Magical thinking is a result in a sense of the child's perception that he is all-powerful, that he causes all things to happen. Such thinking can lead not only to feelings of omnipotence, but to guilt and distress on the child's part. An understanding of magical thinking will help you to comprehend your child's sometimes puzzling reactions to divorce (p. 21).

This magical thinking causes most children of divorce to continue believing that their parents will eventually get back together, even after years of separation. I have observed this phenomenon numerous times, and research has borne out the fact that most kids hang onto an unrealistic fantasy that their parents will someday be reunited.

Magical thinking is most pronounced in children between the ages of four and eight. The combination of egocentric thinking and magical thinking leads to the inescapable conclusion that "my parents will get back together because that's what *I* want."

Billy was only seven but was very mature because of what he had experienced. By the age of four he had witnessed his mother being beaten on a number of occasions. One time he had even called the police and subsequently watched his father being taken away in handcuffs. Even though his parents had been separated off and on over the previous three years, he was surprised when his father left for the last time.

When Billy came to talk with me, he demonstrated a great deal of anger and resentment toward his father. In great detail he recalled incident after incident in which his abusive father had either hurt someone or broken something. Yet when Billy talked about the future, it always included his dad moving home and interacting with the family in a healthy manner.

Was this merely a childhood fantasy, or did Billy really believe that his miracle was going to happen? Young children have a hard time separating fact and fantasy. And adults have a hard time knowing what a child is thinking. Certainly for a child younger than six, there is often a real belief that Mommy will remarry Daddy and they will live happily together. After all, they believe that Santa and the Easter Bunny are coming as well.

After the age of six, children gradually begin to understand make-believe and fantasy. However, many still believe that if they wish for something hard enough, they can probably make it happen—a supposition that is supported by many of our favorite children's fairy tales.

As they develop and become less egocentric, children learn that they can neither control adults nor make things happen by sheer will. They cannot make Tinkerbell live again by wishing real hard. Yet, well into their teenage years, some children of divorce continue to hold onto the hopeless fantasy that their parents will reunite.

Patty was fourteen when she first came to see me for counseling. Her parents had been divorced since she was five. When she was younger, Patty used to see her father every other weekend; but when she was eight, her father remarried and moved about fifty miles away. From that time on she saw her father only during major holidays and for two weeks in the summer. As is usually the case, Patty did not like her stepmother, whom she always referred to as her "stepmonster."

This is how Patty described her magical thinking: "When I was younger, I always dreamed about the day when my mom and dad would get back together and we could be a family again. Then when my dad got married to that witch, I felt like she had taken him away from us. Whenever I went over for a visit, I have to admit that I was kind of a brat. I sort of wanted my stepmonster to be miserable so that she would leave and then my mom and dad could get back together again. Now I realize that will probably never happen. In fact my mom told me that she and Dad wouldn't get married again even if he and my stepmom got a divorce. Still there are a lot of days that I think I wouldn't have had so many problems if only my parents had stuck together."

Even divorced adults can retain some aspects of magical thinking. They live with the expectation that their ex-spouse will return, repent of all wrongdoing, and beg to be taken back. Or some may live for the day that Mr. or Ms. Right will come along and rescue them from a lonely life.

Is this just wishful thinking? Perhaps. But there is just enough little kid in all of us to keep our hopes alive. We need to be careful that we face our fantasies for what they are. Otherwise we will be left even more disillusioned, lonely, and despairing.

Summary

As we have seen, concrete thinking, egocentric thinking, and magical thinking combine to cause the child of divorce to have untrue beliefs and unrealistic expectations concerning the divorce and their future. Some of the results are that they feel all alone, focus only on *their* heartache, blame themselves for some aspect of the breakup, and hold onto the belief that someday their parents will get back together.

Next we will begin to look at the reactions of children who are experiencing the breakup of their parents. Now that we better understand the way our children think, we will be able to view their reactions through the eyes of a child.

Part 2

Your Child's Reaction

Typical Reactions

Bobby was sound asleep when his mother shook him awake. "Get up, Bobby! Grab your blankie and teddy bear. We're going bye-bye."

The boy, who was only five-and-a-half years old, quickly grabbed his things as his mother whisked him away in the middle of the night. He remembered very little about that night beyond that point, as he drifted in and out of sleep. His mother took him downstairs, loaded him into a car full of family belongings, and drove off to Bobby's grandmother's house at the other end of town.

As Bobby woke up the following morning and saw that he was at his grandmother's, he realized that he hadn't been dreaming about the night before. He was glad to be at his grandmom's but was a little confused as to why they left so abruptly.

Bobby asked his mother all kinds of questions as they sat around the breakfast table. "Where is Daddy? What are we going to do today? When are we going home?"

His mother's evasiveness and tendency to change the subject only caused Bobby to be more confused and curious.

Later that same day as Bobby was being put to bed in his grandmother's spare room, he once again asked his mother, "Where's Daddy?" and "When are we going home?"

His mother looked down at the floor and said, "I don't know where Daddy is and I don't know when we're going home."

Bobby, who was pretty smart for his age, was now very confused. He knew that there was something wrong. Mom was acting funny. Grandmom and Grandpop were acting differently, and this wasn't like the typical visit to Grandmom's house. Daddy wasn't with them.

He soon began to wonder, *Did I do something wrong? I wonder if Mom or Dad is mad at me? Well,* he reasoned, *at least I haven't been yelled at or punished, so maybe everything will be okay tomorrow.*

The days came and went with some days seeming almost normal. But most days Bobby wondered, *What is going on with my family, and why isn't Daddy around?* The more he asked questions, the more his grandparents and his mother seemed to avoid giving answers.

Then one day, after more days than Bobby could count (several months), his mother came to him and said, "Bobby, sit down. We need to talk." Mom began to explain that she and Daddy were not going to live together anymore. She talked about their fighting, about their not being in love anymore, but Bobby didn't understand any of that. He only remembered that his mother said that he and his daddy were not going to live together. Oh, he liked his grand-parents all right, and he liked living there with his mother, but he didn't understand why he, Mom, and Dad couldn't live together again in their old house.

He had lots of questions but didn't know how to ask them. So Bobby only nodded his head and ran off to play. He still wondered what was going to happen to him.

His mother, on the other hand, thought that things had gone really well. She had avoided saying anything to Bobby up until that point because she didn't want to hurt him. Besides, for a long time she wasn't sure whether her separation from her husband was going to be permanent. But after almost three months at Grandmom's house, Bobby's mom had come to the decision that she was going to seek a divorce. She had talked to her parents and had sought counsel from a pastor at the church. She finally concluded that she could no longer live a lie. The hardest part for her was telling Bobby, but once she made up her mind, she knew it had to be done.

When Bobby didn't object, cry, or show any traumatic reaction to this difficult news, Bobby's mom assumed that he had taken it fairly well. She had no idea what was going on inside the mind of her child.

As the months passed, Bobby's mother became more and more preoccupied with her own problems. She had reestablished contact with her husband, most of which was unpleasant. They were discussing lawyers, finances, custody arrangements, and settlements, which all brought about increased stress. One bright spot, however, was the observation that Bobby seemed to be fine. He had found a few friends in his new neighborhood, and he seemed perfectly content with the new living arrangement.

Therefore Bobby's needs and his adjustment became secondary to questions such as: Where are we going to live? How can I support a household as a single parent? Will I ever be happy again? Despite the stress of these issues, Bobby's mother always consoled herself with the thought, *At least Bobby is doing okay.*

That consolation didn't last very long. Bobby's mother had just worked through an arrangement where Bobby could visit his dad on alternating weekends, when things began to change.

Bobby was excited when his mom first told him about the visit to his dad's. However, within hours after that, he began to behave differently. At first Bobby acted very short and cold toward his mom. She just thought, *Well, he must have a lot on his mind.* But soon this distance turned into overt anger, displayed as temper tantrums, talking back, and refusing to carry out even the simplest responsibility. As Bobby began his regular visits with his dad, things got worse. It seemed as though each time Bobby returned from a visit with his father, he demonstrated even more anger toward his mom.

In school Bobby was performing well in first grade. However, as visitation with his dad progressed, his grades began to slip. At a subsequent parent-teacher conference, Bobby's mother was surprised to learn that her son was showing signs of anger in school—fighting in the schoolyard, picking on other kids, and displaying a generally bad attitude toward school.

For Bobby's mom, this was the last straw. She decided to send him to the school guidance counselor so that she could gain some new insights into Bobby's problem. She assumed that his problems had something to do with his father, since she hadn't had any trouble with him before the weekend visits began.

A few months went by, along with several visits to the counselor, and Bobby began to show slow, general improvement in his behavior. His temper tantrums lessened, and the school reported fewer problems. His grades, however, were still low. He was described as being very distracted.

The counselor reported that Bobby was opening up in the sessions and sharing his concerns over his parents' breakup. The visits to Dad were not the cause of his problems, the counselor reported, but rather the insecurity Bobby felt when he went back and forth between the two homes.

A year after the breakup of Bobby's family, he was showing fewer and fewer signs of anger but now seemed more sad and withdrawn. His mother noticed him crying alone in bed a few times. He also seemed very distant and withdrawn whenever his weekend visits were approaching. She assumed that Bobby would work through these problems. After all, he was in counseling, and she had her own concerns to work through.

Bobby's schoolwork remained poor, but at least he was passing. His teachers now described him as being somewhat withdrawn and uninvolved in general classroom activities. Most affected were his reading level and handwriting skills, which seemed to regress as they approached the end of his first-grade school year.

Bobby kept showing mild improvement but would revert to his withdrawn or sullen behaviors around the time of holidays or any kind of special event within the family. He seemed very sensitive to change and was quick to display anger or sorrow.

This emotional roller coaster did not begin to level off until more than three years after the separation of Bobby's parents. By then they were divorced and there was a consistent visitation arrangement that seemed to be working well. Bobby's mom and dad were even talking to each other more civilly. The only change in Bobby's slow and steady progress came when his mother went out on her first date.

Bobby, who was then eight, acted horribly that whole week. And when Mom's date arrived, Bobby was at his all-time worst. He was rude, refusing even to speak to the gentleman. Throughout the following week, Bobby was very angry and rude toward his mother. It wasn't until weeks later that Bobby finally came to his mom and asked a revealing question: "When are you and Dad going to get back together?" His mother used this opportunity to explain once again to Bobby the finality of their divorce and to reassure him of their commitment to his well-being.

Today Bobby is in high school (but call him Bob now). He has the same insecurities and struggles that most teenagers experience. It's difficult for his mother to determine how many of his problems are due to the single-parent home, and how many are part of normal teenage development.

Bob has a fairly good relationship with his mom but rarely sees his dad due to their busy schedules. Bob's grades are back to normal, and he is involved in typical high school activities. The only remnants of his parents' divorce seem to be those nagging questions that he still struggles with, but rarely talks about. These thoughts go through his mind:

- I wonder if my parents will ever get back together again.
- I wonder if I did something to cause my parents' divorce.
- Does my dad really love me, and if he does, why doesn't he visit very often? Is he really too busy?
- Why couldn't Mom stick with Dad just for my sake?
- I wonder what kind of parent and husband I will be, considering the fact that I've never really lived in a "normal" family.

Even though most of these thoughts have already been dealt with, they still lurk in the back of Bob's mind, creating insecurity and a general hesitancy to trust in relationships.

Three Categories of Adjustment

Bobby's example may seem like an isolated case, yet it is fairly typical of those who work through their parents' divorce in a healthy way. A number of studies have demonstrated that most children have similar patterns in reacting to their parents' divorce. (See Joan Kelly, "Longer-Term Adjustment in Children of Divorce," *Journal of Family Psychology,* December, 1988.) These reactions can be divided into three general categories. Children of divorce fall rather evenly into these three groups.

Healthy Adjustment

The first category, making up approximately one-third of the children of divorce, includes those children who come through their parents' breakup and are fairly healthy, as in the case of Bobby. They go through the normal grieving process, experiencing denial, anger, and depression, but usually within two years they reach a point of acceptance. This acceptance seems contingent on their parents' ability to work through an amicable settlement and is most evident when there are few disruptions following the divorce, such as remarriage, a major change in lifestyle, or inconsistent visitation.

Typically there are points of disruption beyond the two-year adjustment period, such as when Mom or Dad start dating or maybe even remarry. Yet this segment of the children of divorce demonstrates a fairly healthy adjustment. In fact two years after the divorce, this group cannot be distinguished from other children whose parents have remained together. Counselors or others very close to these children might recognize the fact that many of them still have persistent questions about their parents' divorce, even five to fifteen years later. Yet to an outside observer, they seem like typical children with normal activities, values, and concerns.

Extended Period before Adjustment

Another third of the children of divorce go through the typical stages of grieving but seem to spend a lot longer at each stage. In particular they don't reach a point of acceptance within a two-year time period but tend to take anywhere from three to ten years. Generally there are more boys than girls in this category, since boys tend to react more strongly and take longer to recover.

This middle group also tends to include children who, unlike the first group, have other family stresses to deal with, other than their parents' divorce. These stresses may include but are not limited to:

- a major move, or major change in lifestyle (usually a drastic decrease in financial status)
- remarriage of one of the parents and/or the blending of families
- a parent's alcoholism or drug abuse or any type of physical abuse from either parent
- a particularly messy divorce, such as a prolonged legal battle or custody fight

This middle category can also include children of divorce who experience delayed reactions to their parents' breakup. These children may seem fine for the first two years after their parents' separation, with little or no noticeable reactions. Yet three to five years later, with the onset of a new developmental stage (such as becoming a teenager), these kids will have a more severe reaction—testing limits, questioning authority, and generally distinguishing themselves as "troubled youth."

The long-term effects are much less noticeable when this group reaches adulthood. They finally do make appropriate adjustments and have fairly normal adult lives. They do, however, struggle with personal insecurities and show some evidence of difficulty with relationships and trust.

This can affect their self-image, their friendships, their marriages, and the way they raise their own children.

Lack of Adjustment

The final third of children whose parents divorce are those who never seem to recover from the traumatic effects of their family breakup. Their anger, depression, and general inability to accept their parents' divorce continue well into their adult lives. This can result in school failure; chronic unemployment; an inability to trust others or to establish long-term relationships; and in the most extreme cases a higher frequency of drug or alcohol abuse, personality disorders, and perhaps even criminal behaviors. Some of these people marry young (and many soon divorce); others seem unwilling to ever get married or have a family.

Mike is a good example of the child who could not adjust. Mike was twenty-seven years old when I first met him at one of our church's social functions. He was friendly but somewhat hesitant in anything other than superficial conversation. As I tried to get to know Mike over a period of several weeks, he peeled away the veneer little by little and revealed more of his real self. As he did, a much different person began to emerge.

I eventually recognized that Mike had a drinking problem—not when he was with me, or with anyone from the church for that matter. He had a whole other set of friends with whom he got drunk and then usually got into some type of trouble. The trouble would start with rowdiness and belligerence, but all too often evolved into fights, breaking windows, and eventual arrest.

I remember the first time I learned that Mike had spent the night in jail. I felt bad for him, but I challenged him: "What's going on? How could you pick a fight with a cop?"

Mike's response was one that I later heard over and over again each time he got into some trouble. "Well, when I was six years old, my parents got a divorce. My dad took off with his secretary, and I didn't see him for three years." Mike would go on to explain how upsetting his childhood was and how unfair it all seemed.

I remember saying, "Yeah, but Mike, that was twenty years ago. Isn't it time to move on with your life?"

Mike's response to my insensitive comment was filled with anger. "You don't understand! Nobody understands what it's like. Each time I get into a fight or take a swing at a cop, I'm getting back at my dad. I'd like to kill him for what he did to me and my mom."

That comment pretty well summed up Mike's excuse each time he was thrown in jail or sent to an alcohol rehab center. Although I continued to reach out to Mike, he began to shut me out more and more, following the pattern of all of his relationships.

I eventually lost touch with Mike for several years. Then I ran into him one morning in a coffee shop. He had the same innocent, boyish grin and once again seemed very standoffish at first. I asked him how he was doing and where he'd been for the past several years.

Mike proceeded to tell me that he had just gotten out of prison for a drunk driving conviction.

"How did that happen?" I asked.

Mike, who was now over thirty, recited a now familiar response: "Well, when I was six years old my parents got a divorce. . . ."

It seems that Mike will never fully recover from his parents' divorce. And his reaction, while probably more extreme than most, is similar in its long-term effects to that of almost one-third of the children of divorce.

Would Mike have had problems with drinking and self-control if his parents had never divorced? Probably. No one can really know for sure. It would seem, however, that the inclination was always there and that the divorce was only a catalyst for the problems. No one knows what other catalyst might have set off a similar reaction or if *any* catalyst would have triggered such an intense response.

Summary

Approximately one-third of the children of divorce exhibit only minor (and healthy) reactions to their parents' breakup. Yes, they do go through their own grieving, but if you were a teacher in a typical classroom, these kids would appear to be no different from the average student.

The second third are children who have a more severe reaction, but eventually (three to ten years later, depending on the age of the child when the divorce takes place) work through their grieving and go on to live productive, healthy lives. If you were their teacher, you would notice a difference in these children, in their behaviors, emotions, or even schoolwork; but if you visited with them five years later, you would consider them well-adjusted.

The final third are children who have severe reactions and never seem to recover from their parents' divorce. Our jails and rehabilitation centers house a very high percentage of adult children of divorce, with some estimates as high as 85 percent. The good news, however, is that two-thirds of the children of divorce work through the trauma of their parents' divorce and achieve reasonably healthy adulthood.

If you are a divorced parent, one of your greatest desires is to see your children adjust as well as they can to the stresses of the family breakup—to be within that first third of the children of divorce. There are many things that parents can do to help their children adjust in a positive way. Later in this book we will explore some of them. But first we will cover the feelings your child is likely to have as she initially adjusts to your divorce.

The Initial Phase

My summer days *couldn't have been more perfect. The iridescent sun was a perfect match with the Caribbean blue sky. I walked on the green grass in my bare feet, looking up at the clear sky, and thought how lucky I was to have all this and to love the world I was living in.*

At least I loved it until the night came. That's when it would start. The kids were supposed to be sleeping soundly and unaware of the whole nightly ordeal. But, with me being the oldest, I heard the same thing every night—the yelling and screaming, the slamming of doors and chairs, and the cry of frustration and anger. Dad would get mad, and Mom would run away crying. I didn't know what to think. Was it me? Or my brother or sister? Were we causing all this trouble? I didn't understand. It was all so confusing.

I prayed for progress or some kind of change in the situation, but I must not have prayed hard enough, because it did not change. Then came the night of real terror. There was a knock at my bedroom door, so I called, "Come in." In walked my mom and dad, brother and sister. My first thought was that I had obviously done something very wrong, and so I said, "Whatever it was, I didn't do it." But instead of laughing, there was only total quiet. My dad was the one who finally broke the silence. He told us that he had something very serious to talk to us about, and we should all listen closely. My brother, sister, and I sat frozen on the edge of the bed as my mom and dad explained to us the horrid situation. When they were done, we knew of the problems we would have to face and the changes we must undergo in this new thing called divorce. My dad was the one who left the next day to live in an apartment. It was arranged that we would see him on the weekends.

From that day on, whenever I went outside, no longer was the sun as bright or the sky as blue. Now reality had darkened the world around me, and I had to learn to cope and live with the consequences of divorce.

—a fourteen-year-old girl

The initial period—just after your announcement to the kids that your marriage is over—is critical. In any crisis, what happens immediately after the blowup is especially significant. I realize it may already be too late for you to undo some things that should not have been said or done, but we need to recognize the impact of those moments to plan how to cope with the later fallout. I also know that the handling of those moments is not entirely up to you. Your former partner may have done or said damaging things. In any case, for many children of divorce, the beginning of the end is the most difficult time, and we need to understand it.

Being awakened in the middle of the night by your parents' fighting, abruptly leaving your home and father on the eve of a special holiday, having to call the police while you watch your father beating your mother, feeling that your whole world is falling apart as you suddenly move to another town without your mother's knowledge—all of these situations have been described to me by children of divorce. Even without such dramatic details, it is an extremely emotional time for all parties involved, and as a parent, you want transitions to go as smoothly as possible for your children.

Since you are most certainly going through your own grieving process, you may be in no condition to address the emotional needs of your children. You may not even think about their emotional needs until months later, and by that time some initial damage may have already been done. So it's essential to seek help from others in this crucial time—family, friends, a professional counselor, or pastor. If your family or friends are as emotionally wrapped up in the problem as you are, then they may not be the best source of help, but you could consult a pastor or church leader or a professional counselor to help you deal with your children's needs.

It's also important for you to know what you can expect from your children as they cope with your divorce. There are some normal reactions that may disturb you, though they are ordinary stages of adjustment, but there are also danger signs.

If your child gets the flu, you know something's wrong. Of course you recognize the obvious symptoms—the child loses energy, has a fever, gets some sniffles. But you don't know how serious it is. Those symptoms could relate to problems that are worse than the common flu, and you want to be careful with your child's health. So you take your sick child to the doctor. On examination, your doctor tells you, "Yes, your child has the flu. There's a lot of this going around right now. Give him lots of fluids and rest. He'll feel better in a few days."

You go home feeling much more relaxed, but what has really changed? Your child is still sick and the doctor has really done nothing to help you. So why do you feel better? Because you found out (1) that the symptoms are normal, (2) that other kids are going through the same thing, and (3) that your child will get over it, just give it some time.

So it is with your children's reaction to divorce. I want to describe to you what the normal symptoms are, assure you that there are other kids going through the same thing, and reassure you that your child will reach a point of acceptance, even though it may take more time than you thought.

The amount of time that it takes children to recover from the trauma of divorce will vary, as will the intensity of their reactions, but the emotional stages they go through seem to be fairly consistent. Researchers have indicated that a child's reaction to divorce approximates the same stages of grieving that adults experience when they lose a loved one through death or the breaking off of a significant relationship. This seems to be true across a wide range of ages, including adult children of divorce.

From preschoolers to adults, there appears to be an instinctive process of grieving. We tend to mourn our losses in the same general way. Yet there are some variations in the way the stages of grieving are experienced and in the speed of the process. Among children, these differences depend on a number of factors, including but not limited to the age of the child, the sex of the child, the way the child relates to both their father and mother, the way Mom and Dad relate to each other, and the stability of the child's environment.

Three Phases

Social scientists have thoroughly studied the human grieving process, focusing on people's reactions to the death of a loved one and on reactions to news of terminal illness. What happens when we suffer the loss of a companion or our own health? Details may differ, but the pattern is strikingly similar. We first pretend it's not happening; then we get angry about it; then we seek ways to fix the problem. When our efforts fail, we get depressed. After all that, perhaps a year or two (or more) after hearing the bad news, we finally accept it.

In my work with people experiencing divorce, I have noticed the same pattern: denial, anger, bargaining, depression, and finally acceptance. That only makes sense— divorce is a major loss too. And of course the children of a divorcing couple face profound loss, sometimes more profound than that of their parents. So we can expect children to go through the same grieving process. If we understand how they grieve, we can know more about how to help them.

The grieving process seems to fall into three phases: the initial phase, the secondary phase, and the acceptance phase. Most children will jump from phase to phase, often regressing numerous times before reaching a point of acceptance. Even when acceptance is the predominant condition (usually two to five years after the marital disruption), children will often relapse into other phases of the grieving process whenever new stresses enter their lives, extending well into their adult years. These "residual" reactions can affect their own marriages, as well as the way they raise their children.

Within the initial phase, which is the topic of this chapter, there are several predominant emotions, but we can sum them up in two basic reactions: *denial* and *anger.* When you see your child displaying anger or denial, you as a parent may be troubled, but these responses are part of a necessary process. This is how your child is handling the emotional crisis.

During the initial onslaught of information regarding the breakup of the family, your child protects himself from this devastating news by avoiding the information. First the child uses denial. He pretends the split is just temporary. Daddy's just on a trip; he'll be back. But as much as your child denies the truth, some information still seeps in so that he is eventually forced to face reality. At that point many children become very angry, using their anger to deflect what they can't deal with.

Sammy, at age five, did just that. When his dad first told him that he was going to be moving out, Sammy acted as if nothing had changed. His dad was elated that the dreaded news was so easily received. But as Sammy's dad unpacked items in his new apartment, he found red Magic Marker scribbled all over several of his dress shirts. When he confronted Sammy with what he had done, Sammy threw a temper tantrum, kicking and screaming at his dad.

Your child may use denial or anger as defense mechanisms, but these behaviors are not necessarily intentional. Defense mechanisms are largely unconscious. In other words, your child does not decide, *Now I'm going to use my anger to keep from getting hurt*. Rather these emotional responses are like a blinking-eye reaction. When something comes too close to the eye, it blinks automatically to protect the eye surface. So it is with the child's (and our own) defense mechanisms. They kick in automatically when there is a threat of emotional hurt.

Let me further clarify. Even though someone is in the initial phase, which is dominated by denial and anger, it does not mean the person won't feel a full range of emotions, including rejection, guilt, confusion, fear, sadness, and anxiety. But deflection is the main point of this phase, and that is achieved by denying the event or railing against it. Let's take a closer look at these two dominant responses.

Denial

Denial corresponds with the initial realization, *My parents are getting a divorce!* For some children this is an insight or conclusion that they reach on their own, due to overwhelming evidence of a problem. For others, their first indication of a problem at home is when Mom or Dad sits them down and tells them the disturbing news. For most, however, it is a combination of evidence within the family and comments that have been made to them by both Mom and Dad.

Whatever the case, children are not prepared to handle the news that their whole world is about to come apart. This initial shock is met with comments or thoughts such as, *This can't be happening to me.* Or, *I'm sure they will work everything out; I know my parents really love each other.* Both of these comments serve to deflect the truth.

Denial is similar to an actual physical shock. In cases of severe physical injury, people sometimes go into shock. There is an instinctive bodily response that temporarily numbs the great pain. The victim may even show a greater level of ability, as when an injured person is able to rescue his entire family from a burning vehicle. It isn't until later that the pain becomes acute and the person realizes the extent of his injuries.

So it is with the child who first learns that his parents are about to separate or divorce. The mind goes into a type of emotional shock that temporarily numbs the pain. I believe that this is a God-given, natural reaction that we as parents should recognize and accept—and maybe even be thankful for. Denial of an emotional blow has its place in preparing the way for eventual acceptance.

Preschoolers

In the example of Bobby (in chapter 3), his mom was pleasantly surprised at how well her son seemed to take the news of his parents' divorce. This is particularly true of preschoolers (ages two to six) who are not at a developmental stage where they can understand the implications of their family breakup. Their concrete and magical thinking tells them, *Mom and Dad have had fights before. I'm sure they'll work this one out too.* Many times they work through their denial, using fantasy play in which they can pretend that everything works out just fine and the family lives happily ever after.

Denial spares the preschooler unbearable pain. You see, for preschoolers, the whole world is their family. They can't say, "Well, at least I still have my friends, or my job, or my church activities," as adults might. How can we expect them to understand and accept when their whole world is about to fall apart?

So don't be surprised if your preschooler does not express any negative emotions. Besides the basic response of denial, children at this age typically cannot express what they are feeling. They usually don't even know what these feelings are. You have to try to understand their feelings by watching their behavior and then trying to interpret what's going on inside.

One interesting reaction was recently shared with me by the mother of a preschool boy. After telling her young son the devastating news of his father's imminent departure, her son responded, "Can I go out and play now?"

The mother was surprised, but the boy's reaction was typical. Many parents report that their children seem to go on as if nothing has changed. The only noticeable difference may be that the children are a little more clingy, especially when the custodial parent wants to go out without them.

School-Age Children

For the school-age child (ages six to twelve), you can expect a similar type of denial; however, you may hear more questions about how their lives will change. At this age children are stunned by the news, but now they have a better intellectual ability to reason and question than they did when they were younger.

With some children (including some teenagers), their behavior may even *improve* during this time. One parent told me that her two children suddenly stopped bickering with one another. They started doing their chores without being told and were generally very well behaved. "How do you explain that behavior?" she asked.

I attribute it to a kind of shock that the children experience. As they try to deny the breakup and their feelings about it, they want to avoid any behavior that will bring reality crashing down on them. They may also recognize the fact that Mom or Dad is really hurting, and therefore they cool it around the house for a while until things blow over. Unfortunately this reaction doesn't last very long. As the denial wears off, the children become aware of their own hurts and begin to act out their own pain. Enjoy the peace while it lasts!

Teenagers

For the teenager, denial may take the same forms as for those already mentioned but may also demonstrate itself through increased activity outside the home. This, by the way, is the way in which many adults handle their denial—by immersing themselves in work or a hobby or by just refusing to think about what is going on.

Teenagers typically seek independence no matter what the family dynamics are like. When they receive the news that Mom and Dad are splitting up, many teenagers begin to seek excuses to get out of the house. Whether it's a ball team, a church youth group, or a new intense friendship, your teenager may seem to vanish to avoid the pain at home that he's trying to deny.

One mother of a sixteen-year-old boy recently told me about her son's relationship with his girlfriend. "My son had been dating this girl for about six months. When I told him that his father and I were breaking up, he seemed to lean on her completely. I'm glad he has her but I'm concerned that he's over at her house *all* the time! He eats there, hangs out there, and seems to do everything but sleep there. He was never like that before his father left. Do you think it's because he's mad at me?"

Maybe, but it's more likely that the boy is in the stage of denial. He merely intensified his relationship to take his mind off the problems he has to face at home. This can work for a while, but sooner or later he'll have to face the reality of his parents' breakup.

Adults

We don't expect adults, even young adults (who are no longer living at home), to be affected much by their parents' breakup, but research shows profound impact on adult children of divorce. The same pattern applies as for younger children.

Many times this age group is away from home and therefore less dependent on Mom and Dad. Yet they still seem to go through the same denial that younger children experience. Their way of dealing with the denial is usually to immerse themselves in their work, school projects, or social relationships. Another common tactic is to pretend that the divorce will have no bearing on their lives.

One college student told me, "I'm on my own now. What happens to my parents at this point doesn't affect me. I'm more concerned for my little brother."

This same student later dropped out of school, partially due to grades but also because things at home were "falling apart." Whatever the reason, the truth was that he *was* affected and had a lot to work through before he could go back to school.

Then there are the adult children who are married and have families of their own. When they hear about a parental divorce, they tend to react with the same disbelief. Many times they fall into the role of parenting their parents (as do some younger adults and teens), trying to mediate the conflict. Although this may be a natural reaction, parents should not encourage their adult children's nurturing instincts, since this is an unhealthy family pattern. Instead, adult children of divorce need to care for themselves and their own families. Divorcing parents should assure their children that they will seek the help they need from a more neutral and appropriate person.

For adults, the denial does not last as long as for children. Since they possess higher-order thought processes and abstract reasoning skills, they tend to become more quickly aware of what went wrong, who did what first, and why things are not going to work out. Their biggest dilemma is usually their loyalty conflicts—which parent to side with, if either. That remains the major issue throughout the rest of the grieving process.

Helping Your Child

Is denial wrong? Not at all! It's a normal, God-given reaction to devastating news. It's what keeps us from going crazy when the news is too difficult to comprehend. Without denial we would be overwhelmed by anxiety. We all use it as a defense mechanism. Children in particular need denial since they have no other way of controlling adults or their actions.

How can you help your children move beyond their denial? The truth is that there is very little you can do. And perhaps you shouldn't even try, since this is a natural defense for working through pain. Give your children time to adjust their thinking, and let the denial run its natural course. Try not to increase their anxiety by reacting in extreme ways.

Children, particularly the younger ones, are not sophisticated enough to figure out that by staying in denial, they can avoid some of the bad feelings they have about the divorce. It comes naturally to them. (Actually we adults, and some teenagers, are more often guilty of clinging to denial intentionally so we don't have to face bad news.) So don't think your child is using denial on purpose. Children move on in their healing when they are emotionally ready to do it. If you create a stable environment as quickly as possible, you can help your child pass through this stage more easily.

Parents can also help their kids deal with the reality by giving them clear, honest answers to all their questions. Trying to gloss over the truth to save their feelings will only help them avoid reality for a little longer, which needlessly extends the healing process.

An example of how you can help your child face reality is the way you celebrate the Christmas holiday. Often, in an effort to make things seem normal, parents will plan to be together with the children. Dad comes over Christmas Eve or Christmas morning so the family can spend Christmas together, just as they always have. Even though this noble effort seems to be in keeping with the spirit of peace and good cheer, I'm afraid it only increases the children's anxiety and feeds their denial. It's not that you are actually lying to your kids, but, assuming your marriage is really over, in a way you are acting out a lie. Acting happy together helps your children hold onto the fantasy that the family will be fine, just as always.

Instead of trying to recapture a past that is no longer part of reality, build new traditions. For example, the children could spend Christmas Eve with Dad and Christmas Day with Mom. The sooner you establish new ways of living, the sooner you and your kids will be able to move on with your lives—and heal.

Anger

As you give your children honest information and avoid "playacting" in front of them, you'll help them realize that the separation and imminent divorce of their parents is a reality that they will have to face. As they do, one of the first feelings that comes rushing in is a fearful insecurity. And this should not surprise us. This is true even for those eager and sometimes overconfident teenagers! It may seem that they want to go out and discover a whole new life for themselves, one that is completely independent from their parents. But what they don't tell you (and may not realize themselves) is that they also want to come home to a safe environment. They become painfully aware of this need once that safe, familiar home life is taken away from them.

Even though we use denial, some realizations inevitably trickle into our inner selves. Once these realizations accumulate to a point where we must face certain issues, we are filled with fear and anxiety. The way most children of divorce handle their fears and anxieties during the initial phase is with *anger*. This is just another tool that we and our children use to protect ourselves from the reality of the situation.

We all get angry when we've been treated unfairly. Children eventually tune in to the fact that their parents' divorce will shake their lives, and they had nothing to say about it. "It's not fair!"

As time goes on, and more of the reality filters through your children's defense mechanisms, they begin to recognize that they cannot make the problem go away through denial. Their fear leads them to the very natural reaction of anger. Once again, all they are doing is deflecting the pain of the situation elsewhere. Sometimes it is deflected toward a person, and other times it is deflected toward the situation in general. In either case, the child avoids dealing with reality by blaming others. The "Oh no, not me!" of denial evolves into the "Why me?" of anger.

One boy said, "It's like when you first hear about it, you can't believe it's true! Then when you realize that it might actually happen, you get mad at your mom or dad or both. You think, *How can they do this to me? It's not fair!*"

This is probably one of the most recognizable and familiar stages. Whenever people think about children of divorce, one of the stereotypes that comes to mind is the child who is the terror of the class or neighborhood—the Eddie Hysers of this world. Even though this stereotype is overstated, it is certainly true that children of divorce typically carry around unresolved anger. The ways in which they deal with their anger depend a lot on their personality, sex, and age.

Sex Differences

In terms of sex differences, it is generally accepted that boys feel and demonstrate anger more openly than girls, though this is not always true. Certainly personality differences can alter this generalization, but across most age groups, one can expect boys to react more angrily than their female counterparts. And even though they may get beyond the anger stage as their predominant reaction, they continue to show signs of anger throughout all of their stages of grieving, sometimes lasting a lifetime. This does not mean that girls do not get angry. Some show more anger than boys. But for the most part girls are better able to express their feelings and therefore may be more adept at resolving their anger. (It's also possible that our culture has taught girls how to internalize their anger, and that explains why we see less evidence of angry reactions among girls.)

One possible exception to this rule of thumb is found in several studies about adult children of divorce. When parents divorce and there are adult children in the house or out on their own, it is usually the female children who have a more severe reaction. Their anger may be more internalized, but nonetheless they seem to have a more severe reaction to the dissolving family. Why? It's probably that males tend to distance themselves emotionally from their families more quickly, while girls tend to be more nurturing, placing more value on family relationships. Therefore when their parents' marriage begins to fall apart, adult daughters feel more compelled to get involved (or upset about their inability to change the situation), while adult sons are more likely to say, "Not my problem!"

Age Differences

Age differences are a bit more complicated than sex differences, due to the diversity of developmental changes as outlined in chapter 2. With younger children (under twelve), anger is often misplaced. That is, they don't always direct their anger toward an appropriate target.

Typically, children express angry feelings to one or both parents but they can also express anger to siblings, any third party involved in the breakup, and, many times, to themselves. The younger the children, the more likely they are to blame whoever happens to be around. So, even though they may be angry at the parent who left, they will take their angry feelings out on the custodial parent.

For all the reasons outlined in chapter 2, children under six years of age will many times blame themselves for their parents' breakup, and therefore will feel anger toward self or *guilt*. The younger the child, the more prevalent the guilty feelings are likely to be. These children believe that all of the family's activities revolve around them, and therefore they can't help but feel that they must have done something wrong. This reaction can be particularly concerning to parents since it can lead to depression, self-condemnation, and, in the worst case, self-destructive behaviors in their children.

Guilt can be a predominant feeling for other age groups during the anger stage, but as your children get older, they are better able to understand your explanations that they had nothing to do with the divorce. In fact research has demonstrated that among children of divorce who are eighteen or older, the feelings of guilt over the parental breakup are almost nonexistent.

Young Children: Preschool and School-Age

How is anger displayed? For the youngest children, aggressive play and temper tantrums increase, particularly when you (the custodial parent) want to go out without them. Or anger may be most evident right before or after the days of their visitation with the noncustodial parent.

One parent recently told me about her "well-behaved" daughter who would turn into a terror every other weekend, right about the time of her father's visitation. The mother asked me whether this was a good enough reason to try to cut off visitation rights, since the child was obviously reacting so angrily to the thought of her father's visit.

I said that this was a fairly typical reaction to the insecurity and anxiety the child feels about the changing of households. This reaction would subside as the child worked through the anger stage and became more accustomed to the visits with Dad every other weekend. There may have been absolutely nothing scary about visiting with Dad (and the daughter was fine once she got there), yet many children have strong angry reactions just before the visit begins. I conclude that this is a reflection of the anger they feel about the situation in general, rather than anger toward a person.

This doesn't mean that there are never times that you may need to look into what's going on while your kids are at the other parent's house. Use wise judgment, but don't jump to premature conclusions just because your children are resistant about going there. It's probably best to seek a professional counselor's advice if visitations continue to be a problem for you and your kids.

Small children are also not sophisticated enough to decide who is to blame for the breakup. This may be particularly frustrating to the parent who wants to be sure the children know how innocent he or she was in the marital mess. Children will tend to blame the one who leaves, since their loyalty will be toward the one who sticks with them, no matter what the circumstances may otherwise indicate. Contrasting with this point is the fact that, even though they may blame the parent who left, they are more likely to vent their anger in the direction of the parent who is present. This is not only because of availability—that parent is *there*—but also because they feel more comfortable about showing their anger to the parent with whom they feel most secure.

I have heard this complaint from many discouraged single parents. One mom recently stated, "I can't understand how my child can stand there and shout, 'I hate you Mommy!' when I'm the one who does everything for her while her father does nothing!"

Try not to be overly hurt or upset by your child's anger. Remember, he is probably just venting his anger over the situation, or may even be using you as a sounding board because he trusts that you won't leave him like his other parent did. One child put it this way: "You've already seen your dad leave, and even though you're mad at him, you want to make sure he'll come back again next weekend. So you take it out on your mom, because you kind of know she'll always be there for you."

This by no means dictates that you, as the custodial parent, have to put up with abuse from your child. Try to understand his hurt and try not to overreact out of your own frustration over the situation, but feel free to punish the child who is behaving disrespectfully or who is verbally abusive. He may be testing you to see if you care enough about him to discipline him. Remember, your child may try almost anything to get your attention, even if the attention is negative. Better to get mom's attention through acting out than not to get her attention at all.

Teenagers and Adults

For the teenager, displays of anger are certainly not foreign. In fact many parents express the following dilemma: "I can't figure out how much of my teenager's anger is due to our divorce and how much is just typical teenage rebellion." Nevertheless, when divorce occurs, many teens show increased signs of anger, resentment, and rebellion.

Unlike their younger siblings, teenagers will try to assess blame, and then may target a particular person with their anger. This is why you may see teenagers refuse to visit or even speak to one of their parents. If the target of the teenager's anger happens to be the custodial parent, then the rebellion and sabotage within the home can become so unbearable that the custodial parent may give up and allow the teen to run free or may send him to live with the other parent.

But the lines of blame in a marital breakup are not always distinct. In these cases, teenagers' anger may be more generalized. This can be evident in their attitude and behaviors toward parents and siblings, teachers and school, the church and God, and at times their friends and themselves.

As I said earlier, teenage boys are more open with their anger and tend to be more aggressive, although both boys and girls can demonstrate their anger through passive means (passive aggression). This can be seen in many teens through their lack of cooperation, moodiness, and ability to create general turmoil for those around them. A good example of passive aggressive thinking was expressed by one teen who said, "I don't get mad. I just get even!"

Ginny was just such a teen. She was fourteen when her father moved out. Within a matter of months, this once

74

compliant child was growing more and more resistant. She started by defying and talking back to both parents. This carried over to some rudeness at school, which prompted a phone call from the school counselor. Next to be affected was her attendance at church. She began to be slow getting up on Sundays, which evolved into a refusal to go at all. Her involvement within the church youth group faded and those friends were replaced with a new set of friends who were described as "questionable" by her mother. All of these changes served to alienate Ginny from family and former friends.

In counseling, Ginny revealed a great deal of anger. Yet the target of that anger did not seem to stay focused. She blamed everyone else for her confusion and growing isolation. This became almost self-destructive as Ginny was now associating only with those who would lead her into more trouble. Indirectly Ginny felt that she was getting back at those who had wronged her, but in fact she was mostly hurting herself. The child who is trying to get even can never get ahead.

"It's not fair!" is a common theme of teenagers who are angry about their parents' divorce. In many ways they are right. It *isn't* fair. And anger is just a natural reaction to this injustice. The real question is: How will your child display anger? As a parent, you cannot keep your children from experiencing anguish, but you can try to help them work through their anger. Acknowledge that their sense of fairness *has* been violated, but explain also that life isn't always fair. This experience may even become an object lesson that the child will use throughout his life.

Guilty feelings during this stage are much less likely for the teenager than for those who are younger. Teenagers are usually too busy blaming everyone else for their problems to feel guilt about something they may have done. In a few cases, however, teenage children of divorce may feel guilt over their parents' breakup, particularly in situations where they have been the focus of difficulties or arguments in the home.

There is little evidence that adult children of divorce feel any guilt at all, but as previously stated, there may be an increased feeling of responsibility to help, particularly among the women. They may try to get involved and are much more likely to feel anger toward the active agent in the divorce (the one who is seeking the divorce). Depending on the maturity of the individual, adults usually manage their anger better than teens or younger kids. Adult children are able to articulate their concerns, and therefore have a better chance at resolving their angry feelings. If they don't live at home, they don't have to deal with the constant tension and are more likely to have a relationship with both parents.

Helping Your Child

How can you help your child work through the anger or guilt? Acknowledge your child's anger and, if it's appropriate, affirm his right to be angry. This allows for more of the reality of the situation to actually filter into your child's life. This can be very healthy!

Encourage the free expression of your children's feelings. If you even suspect that they may be blaming themselves at all, reassure them that the decision to end the marriage is strictly yours (and your spouse's) and has nothing to do with their behaviors or actions. If your children are young, they may not understand this the first time you tell them, so continue to reassure them periodically just to make sure.

If you are the target of your child's angry feelings, try not to be defensive. It is most important that you are able to *listen* during this crucial time. It would be quite natural for you to defend yourself or to even shout back at your child. But, remember, your child is reacting out of feelings of fear and insecurity—a need to be sure he is loved. Angry behavior may even be an unconscious test to see if you will still love him even when he is bad. By listening, we reassure our children that we will not abandon them.

What if it is the absent parent who is the target of your child's anger? Now we come to the really hard part. Once again, you must listen and you must be neutral. *Do not join in and bad-mouth your ex-spouse!* As much as you may agree or think your child would appreciate your reinforcement of his ideas, it's important that you resist this temptation. Oh sure, your child may want your agreement for the time being, but in the long run it will only hurt your child's emotional growth and probably put your child quickly into a position of defending the other parent. It is very much like the old adage: *I* can criticize my family, but *you* had better not try it!

Michael's mother found herself in this dilemma. "Whenever Michael gets back from visiting with his dad he seems extremely agitated," she reported. "He complains about everything. 'Dad did this and Dad did that.' You'd think he hated going to his father's. But when I agree with him and suggest he just not go anymore, he immediately jumps all over *me* and then starts telling me all the wonderful things that he likes about his father. He sure has me confused."

There are some times when helping your children deal with their anger requires you to go well beyond just listening to them or helping them express their feelings. There are the temper tantrums, the long silences when they refuse to speak, and the belligerent behaviors, which seem to push your buttons.

As difficult as it may be, try to ignore the minor infractions and outbursts. And when it is needed, don't be afraid to lovingly discipline your child (see the appendix for books on discipline under Parenting). But above all, try not to be drawn into a fight. To respond in kind will only increase your child's anger and make you feel as immature as your child is acting. Please note, however, you *will* blow it from time to time. This is inevitable. After all, you are going though your own struggles. When you do mess up, tell your child you were wrong and then start over again, trying to model an appropriate way of dealing with anger.

In the worst situations, your child's anger will lead to behaviors that you cannot afford to ignore. Unfortunately teens have many dangerous options available to them at a time when they might not be thinking very clearly. Drugs and alcohol are the most obvious dangers, but other problem areas include school truancy, promiscuous sex, and even criminal activity. If you suspect your child of participating in any such activities, seek professional help as soon as possible. You must take this type of behavior very seriously and try to nip it in the bud. By quickly treating the symptoms, you have a better chance of keeping the problem from getting worse, and you have a greater opportunity to get to the heart of the problem before your child becomes unreachable.

Professional help can come in the form of a counselor or psychologist, especially one who specializes in treating children of divorce. If you are not familiar with anyone like this, check with your family physician, the school psychologist, or a pastor who knows your situation and can make an educated referral.

As in the case of denial, eventually enough truth filters through the defense barriers that our children once again get a glimpse of reality. They realize, unconsciously, that their denial did not work and that their anger only brought them more pain. Gradually they are able to process what is going on in their lives and what is happening to their family. And even though they are still distorting the reality around them, they are now able to deal with it at some level. This indicates that they are moving on to the secondary phase.

Moving On

Denial and anger are not presented here as exclusive reactions that your child will have when first confronted with separation or divorce. Certainly there are many emotions and many reactions. In addition, even though these phases are presented in an orderly, sequential fashion, your children may jump from one phase to another—over and over again. As I said earlier, even though your child moves well beyond the initial phase, don't be surprised to see a regression to some form of initial reaction whenever a new family trauma or change occurs. These regressions are often evident during holidays or anniversary dates of the breakup—whenever your child is reminded of the depth of the loss.

How long does this initial phase last? A child's passage through the stages of grieving his loss is a very individual process. The speed of the journey depends on your child's personality, as well as how easily your divorce unfolds. Now I know that there is no such thing as an easy divorce, but it does help your recovery and the recovery of your children when you and your ex-spouse can work together for an amicable separation and divorce. This will be discussed further in part 3 of this book.

In any case, you have to expect that it will take several months for your child to work through this initial period. It is not unusual for some children to take a year or more to work through their denial and anger. If you find that they seem to be stuck in one of these stages, you may want to seek professional advice. It is also noteworthy that some children experience delayed reactions, as discussed in chapter 2. This delay can be a form of denial in which your child seems to have no reaction at all until a year or more later. Then he seems to just begin the grieving process. This is most likely in the case of very young children (typically ages two to six) who do not understand what has happened or how it will affect their lives. As they grow and develop, they may start their grieving process at a later point.

Summary

When children first hear that their parents are divorcing, they are immediately flooded with myriad emotions but generally react in two basic ways. The first is denial, which is the result of the child's inability to cope with the devastating news of the family breakup. Once your child gains a glimpse of the reality of the situation, fears and insecurities arrive, pushing your child into the next stage, which is anger. This anger can focus on one or both parents or on the situation in general. These initial emotions can last anywhere from a few weeks to a few years, but the typical time frame is from two to ten months.

To help your child move along in the healing process, you must give honest, clear information, encouraging the open expression of your child's emotions. As the truth filters through his defensive exterior, your child will be able to move on to the next phase of the grieving process.

The Secondary Phase

I know when my dad first left, *I was really mad at him. I blamed him for all of the problems in the house, especially when I would see my mom crying. That would make me want to go over to his place and punch him out. But when I was with my dad, I never said a word about how I was feeling. I was afraid he would leave for good. Then, as I started to accept the fact that my parents were getting a divorce, I think I just gave up. I gave up on school, the track team, and on just about everything. I didn't feel like doing things anymore. I spent most of my time just sitting in my room, listening to my tapes.*

—a fourteen-year-old boy

Beyond the initial phase of denial and anger, children usually become very frustrated, because they learn that they can't make the problems disappear by pretending they're not there and because their anger only seems to make the problems worse. These realizations lead children to begin feeling even worse than they did before. They are unable to protect themselves from all of the junk going on around them or from the onslaught of negative feelings. Even though your child has been able to deflect many of the incoming arrows, some painful realizations have managed to filter in and affect her inner self.

In addition, as time passes, your child becomes emotionally stronger and better able to face the pain. Her defense mechanisms ease a bit since she is now better able to handle the reality of the situation. Since more and more of the truth is getting through to your child, she can no longer use deflection to protect herself. This change marks the beginning of the secondary phase.

This new phase is distinguished by the fact that your child's primary way of dealing with the situation has changed from deflection or avoidance to distortion and filtering of information. Now the external input is able to reach the inner self, which means it begins to affect the child—perhaps even causing your child to feel worse. However, the input is distorted by the remaining defenses, such as bargaining, withdrawal, and the distortion of facts to suit the child's interpretation of events. These new defense mechanisms are necessary because even though the child is stronger, she is still unable to deal honestly and fully with the changes.

During the secondary phase children's feelings may be very similar to what they felt during the initial phase—rejection, anger, confusion, sadness, guilt, frustration, and depression. The difference is that now they are handling the feelings differently. Instead of denying their feelings or deflecting them by blaming others, they are now allowing themselves to feel some of them. They are still too fragile to allow themselves to fully feel their emotions, but they *are* able to begin letting some of these feelings sink in.

What new methods does your child use during this phase to handle her emotions? Usually *bargaining* and *depression* are evident. Most experts consider these the next two stages of grieving.

Bargaining

Bargaining is a form of manipulation that your child uses to lessen the pain or to change the situation to make it more acceptable. And depression is a natural emotional reaction that actually deadens the pain or distorts all incoming information.

In this phase some information is still deflected. Even when children have moved on to the secondary phase, sometimes information is still too hard to deal with, or the children regress to the point that they once again deny or react in anger.

The great paradox in this phase is the fact that *even though your child is emotionally stronger, she is probably experiencing more pain.* This is a necessary part of the grieving process. In many ways, your child must hurt worse, or "hit bottom," before getting better. "Bottoming out" is a common experience in recovery of all sorts.

The bargaining stage is probably the most difficult stage to understand and to recognize. Simply put, it is when your child becomes so frustrated with the situation that she tries to find simple solutions to a very complex problem. The complex problem is the fact that her parents are getting a divorce. The simple solutions are the child's feeble attempts to manipulate her parents into a desired outcome.

Younger Children: Preschool and School-Age

For young children, the motivation behind bargaining is frustration. Your child merely wants to make the pain go away, and many times the goal is just to get the parents back together. At early ages, this usually involves fantasy and magical thinking; but for those who are eight or older, actual manipulation of the situation is very apparent.

It is often hard to pinpoint the bargaining stage because there is some form of bargaining throughout all of the stages. In fact, as I describe its symptoms, you may think, *My kids do that all the time.* As with the other stages, what distinguishes this as a distinct stage is the fact that your children will use bargaining as their *predominant* defense mechanism. This usually comes out of the frustration that *my anger, guilt, or sadness only make me feel worse. The only way I'm going to feel better is to get my parents back together.* Or, *Things will only get better if I can help my mom find a new daddy for us.*

Now if these quotes don't sound at all familiar to you, that's because your children do not verbalize these ideas, they only *think* them. Since younger children are not sophisticated enough (usually) to figure out how to make their wishes come true, they only fantasize about their parents getting remarried to each other, and then sometimes will unconsciously act on those fantasies.

Ryan is a very good example of this phenomenon. Ryan's mom and dad had been divorced for about three months.

He had been showing signs of anger toward Mom and toward authority figures at school but was now finally settling down to more normal behaviors. At this same time his mom began to date a man she met at night school. Well, you can probably guess what happened next. Whenever Mom's new friend came over to visit or to pick her up for a date, Ryan behaved at his all-time worst.

Ryan, who was only seven, probably did not think, *Now, let's see how I can sabotage this relationship.* In fact he told me he liked his mother's boyfriend. But what he didn't say—and maybe didn't even realize—was that this new man in his mom's life was a threat to his ongoing fantasy that someday Mom and Dad would get back together.

Another common example of bargaining can be found in Tracy, who at age four knew that if she pushed her mom to the limit right around bedtime, Mom would call Dad to come over and discipline her. Of course, as soon as Dad arrived, Tracy would go right to bed with barely a whimper, which only encouraged Mom to call Dad the next time it happened. This went on a number of times until Tracy's parents realized that the motivation behind the misbehavior was to get Mom and Dad back together for the evening.

Teenagers and Adults

For the older child, the attempts at manipulating the situation are usually much more overt. Teenagers may verbalize their desires and then work behind the scenes when you don't comply with their wishes. I have heard many children of divorce talk about how they relay (or misrelay) messages between their parents, changing the tone or content of the message to accomplish some purpose, usually trying to draw parents together or drive them further apart. I find it incredible to see how often this works and how long kids can get away with this type of bargaining. It seems to work best when parents do not speak but use their kids to communicate to each other, putting the kids in the middle.

Other teens, who are perhaps less devious, will not give misinformation but will give just enough detail, or omit just enough, to convey the message they want heard. One fourteen-year-old girl did this as she told her mom how hurt Dad seemed, how bleak his apartment looked, and how lonely he appeared. Perhaps if Mom felt sorry for him, she would not be as mad.

For adult children of divorce, bargaining usually involves their getting into the middle of things—if not to mediate and get parents back together, then to comfort one or both parents through their suffering. This very difficult role takes its toll, even on adult children. The effects of your divorce can sometimes be just as devastating for your adult children as for you. That is why your children try to do whatever they can to help make the pain go away— just as you do.

Helping Your Child

The best way to thwart bargaining is for parents to avoid involving their children in the parents' relationship. Negotiate with your ex-spouse person to person. If you did not get your support check for the month, don't ask the kids to "just mention it to your father when you see him." The more open your communication with your ex-spouse, the better you will be at co-parenting. And your children will be less likely to believe that they can change their home circumstances through any form of bargaining or distortion of facts.

Bargaining is a lot like denial in that the motivation behind both is to help make the pain go away. And for both stages your part is to help your children deal with the reality they will have to face. It seems cruel to say that you shouldn't sugarcoat the situation to save your children some pain, but the truth is that the sooner your children learn the truth, the quicker they can begin to deal with it and move forward in their lives.

One final note about the frustration and bargaining that children experience: These feelings may not present themselves as a separate stage but may instead be intermingled with other stages, including denial, anger, guilt, and our next stage—depression.

Depression

We have described all of your child's emotional reactions, so far, as defense mechanisms. I know it's hard to imagine depression as a defense against anything, but it can be. Actually, depression is a natural reaction to overwhelming life change and pain. It's like an electrical switchboard that shuts down when it is overloaded with current. This shutdown may create a crisis situation and may inconvenience a lot of people, but without such safeguards the electrical overload could cause a worse catastrophe, such as a fire or explosion.

This kind of depression is referred to as a "reactive depression," since it is in reaction to specific life stresses. This is different from a depression caused by a chemical imbalance, hormonal change, or hereditary predisposition. These latter depressions need to be treated by a qualified professional. (Contact your family doctor for a referral if such a depression is apparent.) But, assuming your child's depression is merely reactive, you need to understand it as a natural and necessary part of your child's grieving. It is also the way your child protects herself from more extensive damage. So in this sense, depression is a defense mechanism.

Most of us reading this section are familiar with the depression and anxiety described in this stage because at some time in our lives we have experienced it firsthand. However, many of us may be surprised to learn that young children get depressed and overly anxious too. I have talked with four- and five-year-olds who have even mentioned suicide as a possible escape from their problems.

Depression usually begins once the reality of the situation sets in. By this I mean that children have moved beyond denial, recognizing that they cannot control their parents or the situation. Their anger and guilt have only made them feel worse, so they give up. They have learned that they are totally helpless to change the situation through bargaining, and therefore must accept the way things are. That's depressing!

Being in the depression stage does not mean that your child will not slip back into anger or bargaining. In fact, as I have said, it is common for people to slide back and forth among all of the stages, like an emotional roller coaster, on a daily basis.

Most of us know how we feel when we're depressed or anxious, but how can you recognize it in your children, especially when they are too young or unable to express how they feel? Childhood depression is different from adult depression because it reveals itself in varied ways. For example, children can show depression through sadness, increased anxiety, distractibility, resentment, sullenness, regression, confusion, lack of interest in social activities, loss of appetite, and even through acting-out behaviors. The way your child demonstrates depression will depend on age and personality.

Younger Children: Preschool and School-Age

For younger children (eight or under), depression can appear as sadness and withdrawal, but for some (especially the boys), it may actually appear as increased activity and acting out. This has been called "masked depression" because it seems almost the opposite of what we regard as typical depression. Even though these children seem to have a high activity level and are quite anxious, the underlying feeling is still depression. They merely cover their sadness with tasks or troublemaking.

If your children are in school, you can expect to see lowered school performance, due to increased distractibility and regression. This regression is an interesting phenomenon where children seem to go backward developmentally. Toilet-trained preschoolers will start having accidents again; others will regress to baby talk, and skills that were once known will seem to be forgotten.

I remember one incident while I was consulting in an elementary school. A teacher came to me and said that she thought one of her first-grade students had a brain tumor. "Brian started the school year knowing how to write his name and all the letters of the alphabet," she explained. "As the year progressed, he began to make mistakes on his last name, then didn't know how to write several letters, and now seems to be able to write only a few letters. Is it possible for a child to forget that much in just a few months?"

My immediate response was, "What's going on at home?"

As we looked into the situation, we found out that Dad had left the family about two weeks into the school year. Since then, there had been a lot of discord in the home.

Regression seems logical when you view the sense of loss from a child's perspective. As they move along, growing in knowledge and independence, suddenly their whole world seems to start falling apart. They immediately begin to go back to an earlier, more comfortable stage of development. This helps them feel more secure. They stay there until they feel comfortable enough to step out again in new directions. As adults, don't we do the same kind of thing? We find ourselves retreating back to our parents' house or taking an easier job or acting more like a teenager than an adult.

In addition to regression, some preschoolers and young children will demonstrate their depression through insecurity and an almost clingy dependence. Your child may seem overly anxious, complain of stomachaches, lose appetite, lose sleep, or develop a school phobia. The school phobia, along with the way she clings to you whenever you try to go out, is really just a symptom of the insecurity and anxiety she feels. *Will Mom leave me too? I wonder if Dad will come back. How will we pay our bills? Will we have to move and will I have to go to a different school? Why didn't God stop this from happening to us?* These and a hundred other questions like them all enter your child's mind, with no apparent answers.

For young children there is little to do but wait for the situation to become more stable and secure. This will take time, time for them to grow up and time for them to see that they can begin to trust again. As a parent, you want to provide an environment that will speed this healing process.

Teenagers and Adults

Depression is more recognizable in teenagers because it is similar to that of depressed adults. As children mature, they gain the ability to express the way they are feeling. This assumes, however, that they are willing to talk to you. Usually one of the by-products of the depression is the feeling that no one understands and no one cares. This alienation is particularly strong in teenagers. The divorce just acts as a catalyst for an extreme, rebellious reaction.

Other symptoms of depression include eating and sleeping disturbances, a very low self-image, expressions of worthlessness and hopelessness, regression to a more immature stage, lowered school performance along with heightened distractibility, social and peer difficulties, lack of interest in activities that were once of interest, and in the worst cases, escaping reality through drug and alcohol abuse.

Fortunately the most severe of these symptoms are the exception rather than the rule. Most preteens and teenagers seem to go on as usual, yet they have a sense of loss or sadness that is only noticeable to those who are closest to them. As a parent, you may sense their increased isolation and sadness. It may seem more like a preoccupation and/or emotional distance than a depression.

This was the case for Jenny. She showed a very slight reaction throughout her parents' separation and divorce. She didn't even react when her father remarried just a few months after the divorce. Her mother thought she was doing well but referred her to me when she noticed that Jenny was losing interest in many of her former hobbies, and her school reported that she was falling behind in her work.

When Jenny first came in, she appeared to be a very mature fourteen-year-old. She talked about how well she was doing with all of the changes in her life, as if she were trying to convince me that she didn't need to be there. As we talked over a period of weeks, she began to talk about her loss. "I was always considered to be 'Daddy's girl.' I had no idea that he had a whole other life with some other family. Now he's married to Pam, who has her own two children.

"He comes around here to see me about every other weekend. But what hurts the most is knowing that he is spending every night with Pam's kids. I'm sure he'll start loving them more and more until he forgets all about me. My life will never be the same!"

You can probably see how Jenny's sense of loss is very similar to that of her mom. Jenny feels like she has been betrayed and replaced. Yet when I asked Jenny why she had never talked to her mom about any of this, she said, "My mom feels bad enough. She cries a lot and I know she feels like she's been dumped. I need to be strong so that at least she won't worry about how I'm doing."

As previously mentioned, boys tend to have a more severe reaction to the divorce than girls. And so it is with depression. During this stage junior high and senior high boys can go through a year or more of distractibility, problems in school, social difficulties, and passive aggression. Just as with masked depression in the younger kids, these older students (boys in particular) can underhandedly try to get back at others as part of their depression.

Matthew, at age fifteen, was demonstrating this type of depression. He had gone through the denial and anger stages. Now, about a year later, he was beginning to settle down and let the reality of the situation sink in. As things at home were mellowing out, Mom was beginning to think that the problems were over. Therefore she was quite surprised when she got a call from the school asking her to come in for a parent-teacher conference.

It seems Matthew had not been bringing in his homework assignments, including several large projects. In addition, he had been cited for being late to several classes and had two unexcused absences. Of course Matthew's mother was shocked by these revelations.

When she confronted Matthew about his behavior, he merely shrugged his shoulders and grunted out non-responsive answers. Over a period of weeks, the situation showed no improvement, so his mother brought him in for counseling.

At first, Matthew was a very unwilling participant in the counseling sessions. But as rapport was built, he began to share his basic apathy about life, and in particular toward his schoolwork. "My parents obviously don't care about me," he said. "My dad's gone, and my mom is always either at work or out with her friends. My needs and concerns are not important to anyone, so why should I care about my schoolwork? Besides, the only time my parents talk to me is when I screw up. So this time I really screwed up! You should hear them screaming now."

It doesn't take a psychologist to figure out that Matthew is depressed and seeking attention. However, he is also mad at his parents and believes that he is indirectly getting back at them by doing poorly in school. He needs to learn how to express his feelings appropriately and then recognize that his performance at school is only hurting himself. (We spent the next five weeks trying to get him to understand that concept.)

For the adult child of divorce, it is sometimes surprising how depressing divorce can be. Many parents think that because the kids are older and maybe even out of the house, they won't be affected. But after talking with dozens of adult children, I know that their parents' divorce sent them into a tailspin. They have reported loss of appetite, loss of sleep, inability to focus attention, excessive daydreaming, lack of ambition, and a general feeling of numbness. When the adult children are still (or back) in the home, they and one parent sometimes end up feeding into each other's pain by discussing the events over and over. One woman reported it this way: "We had a house full of depressed people, mirroring each other's anguish and suffering. This went on for months, until one of my sisters started coming out of it. As she got help for herself, she gave the rest of us the courage to begin looking forward."

Helping Your Child

In time, your children, whatever their age, really do bottom out. They reach a point at which they give up. They stop trying to get Mom and Dad back together. They stop believing that life can go on without adjustments and they basically come to the point where they are ready to face the truth, no matter how hurtful it may be. Once they begin to deal honestly with their situation, they are on their way to a point of acceptance.

Even though the depression stage can be one of the longest and most uncomfortable stages (typically lasting from several months to a year), it does serve several very useful purposes. Let me list a few.

- Since people usually shut down during times of depression, this stage tends to provide your children with more peace of mind than the previous stages. (This reaction varies depending on the child's personality.)
- They probably stop trying to control the situation and begin to accept the situation as it is.
- For the first time, they are beginning to deal honestly with themselves about the divorce and are taking a serious look at how it will affect their lives.

- The depression usually signals the fact that your children are at or near the bottom of the grieving process and therefore are bound to start looking up soon.

It is important to remember that this stage is a very normal and necessary part of the grieving process. As parents, we should not negate our children's emotions nor rush them through the process. Don't say to your children, "Stop moping around. Your father's gone, and the sooner you get used to the idea the better." Give them the time that they need to grieve. You don't want to add to their pain by reminding them about all they have lost, but you also don't want to force them to pretend that all is well when they still hurt inside.

Here are a few other suggestions for helping your children through their depression:

- Encourage them to talk to you about their feelings. Make sure you always acknowledge the depth of their loss.
- Don't be afraid to grieve in front of them, but don't model for them a sense of hopelessness or hysteria. They need to learn from you that it is okay to cry, but they don't need to see you out of control.
- Help your children accept the reality of the situation by telling them the truth. Don't hold out false hope to keep them from being hurt. As discussed before, it's better to answer their questions honestly so that they can begin the healing process. Honesty will also help them as they try to rebuild new trust in you.
- Try to find some healthy activities for your children to get involved in. This could include a hobby, church

activity, or school function that might help your children focus on something a little more positive.

Of course, if the depression persists, you will want to consult an appropriate professional. And if the despair or emotional mood swings seem severe (such as with suicidal thoughts), you need to seek immediate help.

How Long Will This Go On?

The secondary phase can take as much as a year to work through. And the entire grieving process can take two or more years. Once again there are wide individual differences in the amount of time it takes children to reach a point of acceptance. This secondary phase is still considered to be the short-term effects of divorce on children. The longer-term effects are generally thought to be those that occur after the child reaches a point of acceptance, usually two to five years after the actual divorce. These effects will be discussed in chapter 7.

Why does the healing process take so long? Rather than a slow, steady progression of emotional growth, the healing process can probably best be described as "two steps forward, one step back." As we have seen, children move toward acceptance, maybe even reaching that point at times, but then inevitably something happens to send them right back down the emotional "slippery slope." That is why your children will need to go through at least two full years before they become confident in their acceptance.

They need to experience at least two Christmases, two Easters, and two birthdays in their "new family" before they can feel comfortable with their new living arrangement. And this assumes that the transition goes fairly smoothly. If you add on a new marriage by one of the parents, or a relocation, or any significant family change, then obviously their recovery can take much longer.

Summary

As children move from denial and anger, through bargaining and depression, and eventually approach a point of acceptance, they are moving through the secondary phase of grieving. During this process, children often feel worse, even while they are progressing. This paradox continues until they eventually bottom out. Barring any new disruptions, they will gradually move toward acceptance.

As a parent, you can help your children move along in their recovery, as long as you don't push them too hard. You need to expect that the grieving process will take at least two years to complete and that any significant family trauma or change will lengthen the recovery. Providing your children with a warm and stable home environment, along with a consistent, stress-free visitation arrangement, is the best way to help your children reach a point of acceptance.

The Acceptance Phase

As bad as my parents' divorce was, *I know that it has made me the person I am today. I think I've gained a different way of looking at the world. It has forced me to take a more realistic view; life doesn't have to be fair! I know that things will not always go the way I want them to. Therefore, moving on with my life has to be a process of accepting what has happened and trying to make the most of it. In school I don't see too many kids with that kind of attitude, so I figure they haven't had to struggle with anything as difficult as I have.*
—*a seventeen-year-old boy*

All divorcing parents want their children to reach a point of acceptance as quickly as possible. Yet we must remember that the grieving process is a natural reaction that must be allowed to run its course. We all tend to believe we're a little further along than we actually are. And so it is with our children. We want to believe that they are fine, but we are usually premature in thinking that the adjustments are over. This was the case for the Logan family.

Mr. and Mrs. Logan had separated only months prior to my meeting their children. Mrs. Logan brought them to me for counseling early in the separation, not because there were significant problems, but because she wanted to head off some of the more serious difficulties. She hoped that as a family they could recover as quickly as possible.

Indeed, the early intervention seemed to be a big help in that Mr. and Mrs. Logan were able to amicably decide on a custody and visitation agreement. For both of them, the chief concern was consistently the welfare of their three children. In joint sessions with the whole family, the children were informed of the arrangements and assured that they were loved by both parents.

This concerted effort paid off in that parents and children were spared the depth of anger and fighting that most fractured families experience. The children in particular expressed only a little denial early on and then went through a period of anger about their situation, which I would categorize as mild.

Within a period of months, all three children seemed to be moving along nicely in their new lifestyle. There was very little resentment or depression, and, in fact, the children were encouraging both Mom and Dad to go out and find someone new. Mrs. Logan spoke to me at that point about concluding their counseling, since everything seemed to be going so well.

Unfortunately, within a week of that conversation, things began to fall apart. It started with the oldest son, Mike, who was about fourteen. School officials contacted Mike's mother because they were concerned about his lack of effort in school and increasing social withdrawal. On further investigation by the school psychologist, it was concluded that Mike was experiencing a significant depression and was in need of counseling.

One by one, the other two children began to experience similar reactions. All three were back in counseling, but this time to talk about their feelings of loss and sadness. They felt little energy for anything as "trivial" as schoolwork and now were very upset whenever Mom went out, let alone tried to date. They seemed to need additional support and security at home, at a time when Mom was making her own adjustments to a new job and new lifestyle.

We were all a little surprised at how long the feelings of sadness persisted. It seemed that every time things were finally moving along, some disappointment or disruption would set everyone back a bit. This up-and-back-again growth toward acceptance lasted for a good year before the children truly began to get over their grieving.

Two years later, the children were finally moving on with their lives and dealing honestly with the trauma of their parents' divorce. There were still some difficult moments around the holidays, as well as an occasional flash of anger toward Mom or Dad stemming from the divorce. These things happen in all families. But through the process, the Logan children gained the emotional energy to handle each new situation and honestly face the implications of the family breakup on their lives. This is what we mean by *acceptance.*

Coping

The acceptance phase is distinguished by the fact that now the child's defense mechanisms are within the normal range. Instead of deflecting or distorting their feelings, the children are now able to allow new information about the family or the environment to affect them directly. Most information passes through the defensive layers, and is then able to reach the inner self without distortion. This is the way healthy individuals deal with their world. The defense system is still in place, however, because we all need protection at times when information is too hurtful to absorb. We continue to filter and distort some information for the rest of our lives. Yet, when we are in the acceptance phase, we are able to deal honestly with most input from our world and then learn and grow from the experience. This is known as coping. Let's examine how the acceptance phase is experienced within specific age groups.

Preschoolers

In this age group I believe it is very unusual for a child to reach a point of acceptance. Actually, most preschoolers merely delay their reactions until they reach a developmental stage in which they can understand what has happened to them and their family. You see, young children are not aware of the consequences and ramifications of their parents' divorce and therefore cannot deal with them. It will take a few years before they understand how the divorce will affect their lives. Once they understand it and come to terms with this realization, then they have reached acceptance.

This is why many young children who see their parents split up will have a fairly mild reaction the first couple of years. They may even appear to have no reaction at all. Then, when they reach six or seven years of age, they may go through a modified grieving reaction. It's as if they just realized the extent of the problem. Then, as they enter each new developmental transition (school-age, teenage, adulthood), they may experience another reaction due to new realizations of the effects of the divorce.

For example, a child of two may show little reaction at first. Then after a period of insecurity and/or anger, the child may seem to be fine with the fact that he lives with his mother and visits Daddy every other weekend.

But once he enters kindergarten or first grade, he may realize that his family is different from other families. Perhaps he'll miss having his dad around more often and will once again mourn that loss as he reprocesses what has happened to him. This gives the child the opportunity to grieve more completely. That is, he can actually reach a point of acceptance of the family situation, even though it has not changed in years. Children cannot really mourn the loss until they can understand what it is that they have lost.

This does not mean that your child's grieving is over. As we will see in chapter 7, the effects can last a lifetime. The reactions can range from mild to severe whenever the child enters a new stage of life. The transition from preteen to teenage years can provide a whole new set of insecurities. Teenage to adulthood can require additional support needs (as in the classic question, "Who's going to help me pay for college?").

Then, when they begin to think about marriage or having children, there's a whole new set of questions and adjustments that usually emerge. These adjustments, however, are well beyond the scope of a young child's immediate reaction to your divorce. These are considered long-term adjustments and will be discussed more fully in the next chapter.

School-Age Children

For the school-age child there is an increasing awareness of the extent of the loss in his life. Therefore there is an increasing ability to reach a point of acceptance. This does not mean that none of the children who witness their parents' breakup while in this age range will have a *delayed reaction*. Some will. However, many are able to reach acceptance within a couple of years and then honestly handle the minicrises as they occur throughout their lives.

At the lower end of this age range (ages six to eight), children will return to youthful play, fantasy daydreaming, and childlike trust as part of their acceptance. At the upper age range (ages eight to twelve), particularly among girls, children begin to take on increased responsibilities and at times act very adultlike, as their way of coping. You'll need to keep reminding yourself that they're still children. You may be tempted to treat them like adults—giving them more responsibilities, expecting adultlike decision making, and maybe even confiding in them. Foster their independence but don't fall into the trap of robbing them of their childhood.

Other signs of acceptance within this age range may include a restoration of self-confidence and personal security, a return to normal scholastic achievement, the ability to focus on new and/or renewed friendships, and an acceptance of the new family structure so that few if any adjustments are needed when your former spouse visits or calls. Within all of these changes the key ingredient is the fact that your child is now able to cope with the changes in life, facing the family situation with a sense of acceptance and restored hope.

Teenagers

With teenagers it is sometimes very difficult to recognize when they are in acceptance. This is because they are usually going through so many adjustments and transitions that it's hard to figure out when they are being typical teenagers and when they are experiencing anger or depression over the divorce. Therefore it is not uncommon for this age group to experience a prolonged grieving period. This can last until the teenager comes to a point of stability. When you combine the turbulence of puberty with the trauma of divorce, you can see why acceptance can be so elusive.

Some teenagers, however, do make the necessary adjustments. They may continue to struggle and experience pain but they are able to cope with their new situation. Some of the evidence that this is taking place may include:

- Your teenager is able to talk to you or someone else about what he is experiencing. The key element here is that the teen is able to describe honestly and accurately the circumstances and resulting emotions.
- For the most part, forgiveness has taken place, so that even though your teen may know that one or

both parents were at fault, that person is no longer the focus of blame or resentment.

- Even though your teen may not be able to express love, there is at least a reestablishment of a loving relationship—one in which there is a rebuilding of trust taking place. (Some parents would swear that this is impossible until the children reach adulthood.)

- Your teen should show signs of risk taking, such as reaching out in new relationships. Risk taking involves facing your fears or insecurities and moving forward anyway. As a result, knowledge is gained. Parents should notice evidence that some personal growth is taking place, as opposed to regression.

- Last but not least, there needs to be some sign of personal responsibility before your teen can truly be considered to be in acceptance. This does not mean that your child is taking any of the responsibility for the divorce itself, but he needs to move beyond blaming his parents or others for *most* of his problems. Instead, your teen should show signs of at least beginning to take responsibility for his own actions and reactions. Ideally your teen will gain an accurate sense of control over his recovery process. Since this ability requires higher-level reasoning skills, it usually increases as your child develops and matures.

Adults

It may seem surprising, but adults experience the same depth of pain and grieving as children do when their parents split up. Many parents have told me that they chose to wait until their children were older and perhaps out of the house before separating, but they were surprised to find that their children still went through a grieving process, even though they were seemingly a lot less dependent on their parents.

Assuming their lives are somewhat stabilized (which means they are not "twenty-one going on thirteen"), the adult children of divorcing parents tend to recover within the two-year time frame and show signs of acceptance more quickly than younger children or teenagers. The list of signs of acceptance is similar if not identical to the list found in the teenage section. The major difference is the amount of time involved. Since adults are better able to understand adultlike motivations and behaviors, they are more apt to accept and forgive after they have worked through their own grieving. One word of caution, however; your adult children are much more likely to figure out what really happened, even though you may not tell them. They are less likely to see one parent as totally right and the other as wrong. They probably see fault on both sides, even though they may side totally with one parent when with that parent. This is commonly known as "buttering both sides of your bread," or learning political savvy. But this is not necessarily a bad thing, just a natural reaction to being caught in the middle.

Helping Your Child Reach Acceptance

We all want our children to reach a point of acceptance as quickly as possible. This can be somewhat unrealistic in light of the fact that a child's grieving is a natural process, which must run its course. I believe that you can't really speed up the recovery time, but you *can* reduce the pain involved by making some wise decisions. I also believe that you can *prolong* the recovery time by making some poor choices, such as using your children to get back at the other parent, prolonging the hostilities, or dating before you or the children are emotionally ready. These and many other errors of judgment are actually quite common among parents who are divorcing.

It is important for you to keep in mind that *the greatest predictor of your children's reaching a point of acceptance is for you as a parent to reach acceptance first.* You see, children don't typically recover in an atmosphere where a parent continues to get angry or fight over co-parenting issues. They also do not do well in an environment where depression, gloom, and hopelessness are pervasive. Therefore you need to do whatever it takes to make *yourself* healthy and then concentrate on helping your children.

I have heard parents say to me that they couldn't go to a divorce recovery program because they didn't want to spend the time away from their children. Or they say they probably need counseling but would rather spend the money to get counseling for their children, since their kids are their priority. Although I can admire the intention of these parents, I also know that it doesn't help the child to work on recovery issues and then walk into a home atmosphere where there is an unforgiving spirit. Acceptance needs to be modeled to kids *first* from their parents.

This does not mean that you cannot show weakness or vulnerability with your children. In fact some signs of healthy grieving can be very helpful to kids. One single mother recently told me about her struggle not to cry in front of her children. She wanted to appear to be strong and healed, even though she was working through a lot of sorrow.

I told her that I thought it would be good to let the children see her cry. "They need to see the healthy expression of emotion and to know that it is okay. On the other hand," I continued to explain to her, "you don't want to demonstrate hysterical, uncontrollable crying. They can benefit from seeing you struggle a bit, but they also need to know that you are still in control, at least in control enough for them to feel secure depending on you."

Honesty seems to be a key in the expression of your emotions with your children. Explain to them how you are feeling and where you are in the recovery process. Don't tell them you are in acceptance when you know you're not. You don't want to lie to yourself or to your children about where you are emotionally.

You may, however, want to push yourself a bit for the sake of the kids. By this I mean you may want to give in or give up on some of your own issues (for example, the need to get even), so that everyone involved can get on with their lives. This is good for you as well as the kids.

A good example of this is the Morgan family. There is no question about the fact that Mrs. Morgan had been dumped. She had put her husband through medical school, and when he was becoming a prominent doctor, he left his wife for a younger woman. This is an unfortunate, yet all too common, scenario. I can empathize with Mrs. Morgan's hostility and desire for vindication. Yet when she and her two children arrived at my office some two years after the breakup, I was struck by how destructive *both* parents had been to their children. They had returned to court several times over custody and financial battles. And now, once again, Mrs. Morgan was thinking of going to court for more support.

After talking extensively with her two children, I recognized that they had both suffered *extreme* heartache because of their being used as pawns in most of the legal battles. Even though their parents desired to leave them out of it, the kids inevitably heard the venom that each side was preparing to use during the next legal round.

Seeing the amount of time that had passed (two years) and the devastating effects on the children, I recommended that Mrs. Morgan examine her motives for going back into court, and try to avoid the litigation if at all possible. As we discussed the matter further, it became obvious to both of us that she needed to let go of her need to make him pay. I assured her that both she and her children would be better off.

As you move on with your life, and especially if things begin to go well, you will begin to recognize the value of forgiving your ex-spouse. Forgiveness is necessary whether or not the other party asks for it. In fact, for the majority, there is never a time when the "erring party" comes back, tail between legs, begging for forgiveness. No, that only happens in your dreams. The truth is that we need to forgive the other party in spite of their actions toward us because it is what truly sets us free to move on with our lives. And for the sake of our children, we need to move on! (See suggested books in appendix under Divorce Recovery.)

The true test of forgiveness comes when you're not doing well, and it seems that your ex-spouse is prospering. Then even the most kindhearted soul steams inside, fantasizing about how to hasten the ex-spouse's downfall. I'm reminded of the single parent who told me that she loaded her kids up with sugar and caffeine before sending them over to visit with their dad and his new wife! (I hope I haven't given you any new ideas.)

Since it is inevitable that these feelings will continue to haunt you, your decision to forgive must be ongoing. In other words, you must continually choose to ignore or let go of those nagging concerns. Your children will see how you choose to handle the minor crises that come up and will learn appropriate responses to life's traumas.

Summary

This last stage of adjustment—acceptance—can take two years or more to reach. We have defined this stage as the point at which your child is able to deal honestly with the new post-divorce lifestyle and begin to move forward in new directions. This adjustment is different within various age groups but is universally marked by the child's ability to be satisfied with the new situation. His defenses are lowered, and he is able to begin taking risks again in significant relationships.

Again, I must say that once children reach acceptance, it does not mean that they will not slip back into another period of adjustment. In fact it is typical, particularly for younger children, to go through all of the stages of grieving each time they enter a new developmental stage or significant transition in their life. This is considered by many to be a "delayed reaction" or just part of the long-term effects of the divorce. These long-term effects are the subject of the next chapter.

Long-Term Effects

Cindy had problems with relationships. She had broken off four "serious" relationships in two years. For each of them, the pattern was always the same. Cindy and her boyfriend would grow closer and closer until there came a point where some type of commitment was implied. Then the difficulties would start. The specifics were different each time, but the basic issues were always the same.

Cindy's partners couldn't be trusted, at least according to Cindy. You see, she would usually set up some type of trap in which she tested the character of her boyfriend. Sometimes it would be checking and re-checking his whereabouts, even though he had told her where he would be. Other times it was asking whether or not he could account for all of his time when asked, "What did you do today?"

I can remember one specific incident in which Cindy was incensed by her boyfriend's "dishonesty." It seems that when she asked him about what he had done that day, he failed to mention that he had called for her earlier in the evening and talked briefly with her roommate. From that point on, Cindy became suspicious that there was something going on between her boyfriend and her roommate. Of course the relationship did not last much longer, and her relationship with her roommate suffered too.

At the age of twenty-five, Cindy came in for counseling, hoping to find out why she seemed to have such poor luck in relationships, particularly with men. As you may have guessed, Cindy came from a divorced home. She first found out about her father's indiscretions when she was about ten. Her parents did not divorce right away, but Cindy remembers a series of incidents in which her mom and dad had prolonged arguments over suspected affairs. Finally, when she was seventeen, Cindy's parents got a divorce, and Cindy saw her father a couple of times a month after that. Her mom continually reminded her of how devious her father had been.

This is a typical example of a divorce that has long-term implications. Today more and more is being published about the long-term effects of divorce on individuals. In the introduction, I discussed Judith Wallerstein's book on this topic. My main problem with her study, which traces the effects of divorce on a small sampling of children through several decades into adulthood, is that it offers little hope. Reading her books, you get the idea that children of divorce are doomed forever. The whole point of my book is that you can avoid that doom if you know the dangers and prepare for them.

Still, Wallerstein's work is helpful in assessing the long-term dangers. She was one of the first to study this, and by now many other children of divorce have stepped forward to tell their stories. I've been hearing these stories for years, both in my counseling practice and in divorce recovery seminars. Divorce has a significant long-term impact on people's lives and relationships.

In fact one of the greatest proofs that I have found for the impact of divorce on children comes from my discussions with adult children of divorce. Every one of them, and I've talked to hundreds, has said, "I'll do everything I can to be sure I don't do this to my children," or words to that effect. The sad truth is that children of divorce actually have a slightly higher divorce rate than the rest of the population.

For people who have come from dysfunctional families, there is huge interest these days in support groups. These groups most frequently include adult children of alcoholics or adult children of incest and abuse. But now more and more we are seeing adult children of divorce meeting together for mutual support. At our own counseling center, just the mention of such a support group will usually initiate many calls of interest from potential participants. As one caller recently stated, "I know that my parents' divorce and the following years of conflict have affected me. I'm not quite sure of all of the ways I have been affected, but I'd love to talk to others who have been through the same type of experience. Just to know that I'm not alone in my feelings and to gain insights into some of my behaviors would be well worth it."

Long-Term versus Short-Term

Many would ask, "What's the difference between the long-term and short-term effects of divorce?" As discussed in previous chapters, the short-term effects of divorce are those reactions that begin immediately and can last for a number of years. The short-term reactions don't truly end, however, until the child reaches a point of acceptance. Beyond that, even though children have worked through the grieving of their family breakup, they still have to work through the implications of growing up in a single-parent home. These effects, the long-term effects, have been documented to last up to fifteen years for some adult children of divorce, and may very well be permanent.

In chapter 3, I discussed the three main categories of reaction for children, and I mentioned that approximately one-third of the children of divorce never seem to recover from the trauma of their parents' divorce. These are the most seriously affected of the children of divorce, both from a long-term and short-term perspective. For the rest of their lives, these children tend to live with the reactions we saw in chapters 4 through 6. They don't learn healthy coping skills, and therefore lead a lifestyle of continuing struggle, depression, anxiety, difficulty in personal relationships, and other problem behaviors.

The children who, after a period of adjustment, are able to cope and move on with their lives (approximately two-thirds) are the ones who seem quite normal to those around them, and outwardly lead healthy, productive lives. Yet (as is true for all of us) what they grew up with greatly affects how they live today. Divorce shapes our personalities and character, our interests and ambitions. Each person is different, and the long-term effects of divorce will be different for each child of divorce. Here I will discuss some general observations.

Factors to Be Considered

There are a number of factors that determine how your children will be affected by your divorce over the long term. Let me list a few of the more influential ones.

The age of the child at the time of the divorce. Researchers estimate that most of your child's personality is developed by the age of six. This does not mean that there are not changes in her personality beyond that time, but for those children who witness their parents' breakup at a young age, there is a greater chance that it will have an effect on their personality. It stands to reason that the longer your child lives in a single-parent or blended family, the more likely it will affect her personality. This does not have to be a frightening statistic if you have young children. It merely indicates that you will need to be even more aware of how your child may be affected, and how you can compensate for specific losses. (*Note:* Most of the longitudinal studies have started with young children and therefore may be overly pessimistic, since these children have spent a greater percentage of their lives in a single-parent home.)

The number of changes that result from the divorce. As I said earlier, the impact of divorce on children is greater when you add on other life stresses, such as moving to a new home, new church, new school district, adding a new spouse to the picture, or trying to blend a family. All of these changes are difficult for children if they are experienced by themselves, but when they are heaped together, as is the case in many divorce situations, there can be lifelong effects. Wherever possible, parents need to control the number of changes and perhaps even make sacrifices to limit the upheaval.

The adjustment of the custodial parent in the divorce. While both parents are of key importance in the eventual well-being of the children, research indicates that the emotional health of the custodial parent is the greatest predictor of the children's adjustment. Therefore, it is important for both parents to get the help they need to resolve the anger, resentment, depression, or anxiety produced by the divorce and to end any ongoing squabbles as quickly as possible. Almost all couples have conflicts during the early stages of the divorce, but if these continue beyond the actual divorce settlement, they can suck all participants back into the black hole of divorce for more years than is necessary.

Since the children spend the majority of their time with the custodial parent, it stands to reason that this parent's attitudes will influence the children. No matter what the circumstances, the custodial parent must choose an attitude of reconciliation, desiring whatever is best for the children, particularly when it comes to the relationship with the other parent.

The relationship with the noncustodial parent. For years we have tended to ignore the importance of the relationship with the noncustodial parent. Within the past five years or so, we have seen more and more research that points to the fact that the noncustodial parent is also a key player. (So if you are a noncustodial parent thinking about giving up on seeing your kids, please read this very carefully.) Many researchers have found that a primary reason for the negative effects of divorce on children is the loss of contact with one of the parents. And in fact the traditional visiting pattern of every other weekend has created feelings of intense dissatisfaction and, at times, reactive depression among children, particularly the boys.

Consistent and frequent contact with the noncustodial parent has repeatedly been shown to correlate with well-adjusted children, unless that parent is abusive or otherwise unfit. Since mothers usually have custody of the kids, I want to point out the importance of maintaining the children's contact with their father. In studies the father relationship has been linked positively with identity with the opposite sex for girls, ambition and motivation for boys, and overall adjustment and relating abilities for both sexes. The well-being of the child has proven to be particularly strong when the custodial mother encouraged continued contact with the father.

If the relationship with the noncustodial parent is so important, then why is it so rare? Research shows that, two years after the divorce, less than half of noncustodial parents have regular visits with their children. This is an alarming and discouraging statistic. I've talked with a number of noncustodial parents, mostly fathers, who have actually given up on visiting their kids. Most of them expressed discouragement over their lack of input into the child's upbringing. To put it in their words, "Why should I continue visiting with my children, when I have little or no say in how the kids are raised?" This is perhaps the reason that joint custody arrangements have a much higher rate of involvement by the father. When they have more input, fathers are more likely to stay involved and, therefore, more likely to have well-adjusted children.

Other specific traumas that accompany the divorce. The research for this is incomplete, but it is my opinion that most of the children of divorce who fall into the one-third of the children who never seem to recover from their parents' divorce are also the ones who have to contend with other specific traumas. These traumas include but are not limited to physical abuse, sexual abuse, severe emotional or verbal abuse, extended neglect, drug or alcohol addiction of one or both parents, and mental illness in the family. For children exposed to these factors, the long-term implications of divorce are greatly complicated by preexisting conditions and compounding problems. Once again, this is a general statement. I'm not implying that your child will be a basket case if she has been exposed to one or more of these traumas. This factor merely indicates a greater propensity for long-term problems and, therefore, the need to be particularly sensitive to the child's needs and emotional condition.

Negative Effects

Diminished Motivation

Jason, who is now twenty-four, first came to see me when he was fifteen. At that time he had long hair (which was a little more in style then), torn jeans, a punk rock T-shirt, and a sour look on his face. Jason was actually referred to me by his mom because he had decided to drop out of school. Mom said she would permit it (she had actually lost her ability to control him anymore) if he would go to three counseling sessions.

Imagine yourself in my position. Here's this big, fifteen-year-old punk rocker sitting in my office, glaring at me as if to say, "I dare you to get through to me." He didn't want to be there, and, to be honest, I didn't either.

Every topic I brought up was met with silence or an occasional "yep" or "nope" (mostly "nope"). Finally, I decided that my only option, and one that I found would work as a last resort, was to talk to him about something *he* was interested in—music. Not just any music, but punk rock and heavy metal music. Now you have to understand that I never listen to punk rock or heavy metal music. In fact I encourage parents to keep it away from their kids. But in this case, I felt it was my only way to connect.

Suddenly Jason became very animated and talkative. He was surprised that I had shown any interest. (Believe me, it was tough.) He later stated that no other adult had ever taken interest in this topic, which he valued so highly. Adults usually walked away or told him to turn it off. Jason went on to tell me about all the groups, the most popular songs, and the meaning behind the lyrics. (As if anyone could actually hear the words.) He then offered to bring his tape player next week, along with a couple of his favorite tapes.

Well, I survived his tapes, and to make a long story short, Jason continued coming, by choice, for the next six months. During that time, he began to tell me about his family, his life, and his feelings. Jason was a very angry young man. His father had left the home when Jason was about nine years old and moved in with another woman. The new woman had children of her own and was soon pregnant with Jason's soon-to-be half brother. As Dad gradually broke off contact (and financial support) with his former family, Jason felt more rejection, resentment, and then anger with each week. He eventually withdrew emotionally, isolating himself in his room with his music and an occasional marijuana joint. Jason's main problem was his attitude and motivation. He had given up on life by the time he was fourteen.

After all, life wasn't fair, and he couldn't even sustain his father's love.

The child's inability to have a sense of control over his own life is what researchers have identified in approximately 45 percent of the male children of divorce. As in the case of Jason, when children are intelligent and talented, there is an even higher tendency for them to show little direction or purpose in their lives. Dropping out of school, not attending college or bumbling their way through college, and being underemployed after school are all typical signs of the phenomenon in male children of divorce (and a few females).

Today Jason works in a factory. He finished high school but went no further even though he has above-average intelligence. He is socially active and appears to be much happier today. His hair is still long, but his taste in music has moderated. To his friends, he's an average twenty-four-year-old and a nice guy. But to me he is a victim—a victim of divorce.

The "Sleeper Effect"

Alice is a twenty-six-year-old adult child of divorce. Her parents split up when she was seven, and she gradually lost contact with her father over a period of two years. Her mother remarried within that two-year recovery period but was divorced again when Alice was eleven. Since the second divorce, Alice's mom has had a series of boyfriends, but has not remarried.

After a period of adjustment following each divorce, Alice seemed to come through fairly well. As is often the case, Alice began to have difficulties in adolescence. She found her first "true love" when she was fifteen and was convinced that they would eventually marry. When that relationship broke off, Alice, in disgust, found that she could use sex to get boys to do what *she* wanted. Throughout high school and college, Alice was sexually active. Soon after graduation, however, she had a born-again experience, which led her into a new lifestyle. She became active in a church singles group and now believes in a heavenly Father who loves her unconditionally, for whom she does not have to perform. The new difficulty is finding that same kind of loving relationship with a man.

Whether it is the reaction found in Alice or the lack of trust found in Cindy, whom we met earlier in this chapter, researchers have documented this "sleeper effect" in approximately 66 percent of the female children of divorce. It's a sleeper effect because it's often found in women who seem to have recovered quite well. It occurs most frequently at a time when women are making important decisions about their lives. In this way it is similar to the diminished motivation reaction in young men.

The common element in the sleeper effect, as seen in Alice and Cindy, is fear—fear of commitment and fear of betrayal. For some, the fear may lead to the coping strategy of control. In other words, "If I can learn how to control men or the situation, then I won't be hurt again." I have seen this numerous times in the lives of adult children. While I can empathize with the feeling, I'm afraid the coping strategy can become quite unhealthy.

Another coping strategy, used by both men and women who are experiencing the sleeper effect, is avoidance. This can include avoidance of relationships or avoidance of any kind of commitment. Usually patterns of relating are developed and unconsciously repeated; relationships reach only a certain level and then self-destruct before they can go any further. These patterns may include an inability to communicate deeper than on a superficial level, an inability to make a commitment, or an inability to allow the relationship to grow beyond a friendship or one that is purely sexual.

The combination of control and avoidance can reach extreme levels among some adult children of divorce. This is evidenced by a disproportionately high number of both men and women who are sexually acting out, homosexual, in treatment facilities for personality disorders, and who experience divorce in their own marriages in spite of vows that it will never happen to them. Without insights into their pattern of relating, and help in overcoming these patterns, these difficulties may follow them the rest of their lives.

The Overburdened Child

Another documented long-term effect of divorce is commonly referred to as the "overburdened child." When a marriage breaks down, it is common for both the mother and the father to do less parenting. The mother (usually the custodial parent) is often worn down by the changes in her life, including moves, job changes, new financial responsibilities, and parenting alone. The father (or non-custodial parent) feels guilt because he is not there for the kids as often as he'd like to be, and he just wants his times with the kids to be enjoyable. Both parents may also be struggling with their own reactions and recovery. Therefore the parents tend to discipline less, spend less time with their children, and be less sensitive to their needs.

Unable to meet the challenges of single parenting, many parents begin to lean on their children to pick up the slack. We have all heard of latchkey kids, who must come home to an empty house and take on major responsibilities in the home well before they might otherwise have to. The child's role may include housekeeping, babysitting younger siblings, being the "man of the house," becoming the mediator in arguments, being the parents' confidant, and emotionally supporting the parent. While most of this is not intentional, it is a fact of life in many single-parent families.

The first time I met Sarah, I was amazed at what a responsible, mature child she was at only fourteen. Her mother was quite proud of the fact that teachers and friends all commented on what a good job she had done raising her daughter all alone. The presenting problem was that they were having difficulty in choosing a college. (Most kids are not even thinking about college at age fourteen.) Even though it was early, Sarah was anticipating a problem when it came time for her to go away to school. You see, she wanted to go *away* for school. Her mother, on the other hand, felt that she should stay home. That way, mom could continue to provide the proper guidance to her daughter.

Since college was still three years away, and Sarah was such a responsible girl, I was confused as to why this was such a burning issue. As we explored it further, it became evident that the reason Mom needed Sarah to stay home was to help Mom "keep it together." Sarah was the one who kept the house in order. She prepared the evening meal and then would ask Mom all about her day when she got home from work. Sarah did not go out socially because she didn't want her mother to be all alone at home. If Mom happened to go out on a date, which was rare, she always solicited Sarah's approval of her choice of a date, because, she stated, "Sarah's a better judge of character than I am." When she returned home from her dates, she would confide in Sarah everything that she liked and didn't like about the person so that together they could come to some conclusion about any future relationship. If Sarah went away to college, neither one of them was sure that Mom could make it on her own. Talk about role reversals!

Sarah is a good example of the overburdened child. The child's role becomes instrumental to the well-being of the parent. The divorce itself may not be to blame but serves as a catalyst for bringing to the surface specific emotional difficulties. As with any type of dysfunctional family, when a child takes on too much responsibility early in life, there will be one of two results. Either she reacts by going the opposite way and becomes overly irresponsible, or she continues in her overburdened lifestyle and therefore runs the risk of perfectionism, nervous breakdowns, being overly nurturing in relationships, overparenting her children, and losing her own identity in the lives of other people. (See suggested books in the appendix under Relationships.)

Preliminary studies have indicated that approximately 15 percent of the children of divorce are overburdened. But some think this estimate is low, since there are increased responsibilities for nearly all of the children of divorce. As we shall see in the next section, a balance of responsibility may be the key, since increased responsibility can actually have a positive impact on some of the children of divorce.

Whether it is diminished motivation, the sleeper effect, or the overburdened child syndrome, it is hard to point the finger of blame only at the divorce. Divorce never stands alone as a one-time traumatic event but is experienced in a continuum that begins with an unhappy marriage, goes through custody battles and court hearings, and results in ripple effects that continue for generations.

Exodus 20:5 comes to mind where it says that the sins of the father are passed on through many generations.

Do these predictions of gloom mean that parents should stay together for the sake of the children? Even though the research is troubling and needs to be taken seriously, there are situations in which continuing the marriage would be intolerable. And to stay in a bad situation for the sake of the children would probably only lead to more resentment and possible violence. Even though there are very few comparisons of children from single-parent homes with children from unhappy, two-parent homes, all known evidence points to the fact that children exposed to parental fighting and the pressure of relentless conflict turn out to be less well-adjusted than the children of divorce.

If divorce is undertaken with thoughts of the children's well-being, and if both parents work together for the sake of the kids, then there are many things that can be done to lessen the negative effects of the divorce on the children. These practical guidelines will be the focus of the next section of the book, but first let's look at some positive things that some children of divorce may experience.

Positive Effects

It is hard to believe there could be anything positive to say about divorce. In fact, in reviewing the literature, it is hard to find anything of a positive nature. But if divorce is viewed as a handicap to children, then we must look at the fact that many people have taken the worst kinds of handicaps and used them to build character and personality that become the envy of others. So it is with the long-term effects of divorce. I have met with many teenagers and adults who have shared how their parents' divorce has built strength of character and moral resolve into their personalities.

As Janet, a sixteen-year-old child of divorce, explained it to me: "It is hard to find anything positive that can come out of the divorce when it first happens. My dad left when I was only six, and I know that it has been difficult on me and my mom. But I wouldn't trade anything for the things that I have learned from growing up in a single-parent household. I have been forced to face the realities of life at an early age, realities like life isn't always easy and there are no guarantees in life. These things have forced me to be more practical and down to earth. I know that I'm a more responsible and resourceful person today because of the divorce."

Crystal, a seventeen-year-old, expressed similar thoughts: "Yeah, it definitely takes time, but you do work through it, and when you do, you find that you are much more understanding than other kids your age. You have to be! After all, you've seen your parents fail. Everything they taught you has fallen apart. So now you have to decide how you're going to live your life. What are you going to believe in? For me, it has strengthened my faith in God. He is real in my life, not because my parents told me so but because I needed a source of strength that was greater than me and greater than my parents. I've found that now, so I consider myself luckier than other kids my age."

David, a seventeen-year-old survivor of two divorces, put it this way: "Something about the divorce forces you to view life differently. It somehow puts every other life event in perspective. When your mom or dad leave you at age five, and your whole world seems to fall apart, then you are better able to deal with other crises as they occur. You're perhaps wiser and more mature. For example, I see some of my classmates who fall apart over bad grades or College Boards or something. You even read about kids who kill themselves because they didn't get accepted to the college of their choice. Things like that upset me, but I know it's not the end of the world. I always figure to myself, *You've survived your parents' divorce, you can certainly get through this one.*"

Here are some of the common themes that I have heard when interviewing children of divorce about the positive aspects of divorce. First and foremost, they all indicate that there is *nothing* good about it in the beginning. But over a long period of time, some of the following characteristics may emerge.

Children of divorce are more sensitive to other kids and their problems. It stands to reason that when you've been through a significant life trauma and have felt as if no one else understands your pain, once you work through that, you are bound to be more compassionate with other people and the difficulties they face. I have seen this first-hand whenever our counseling center sponsors a program to help others who are struggling with some life crisis. Adult and teenage children of divorce are among the first to volunteer to help.

Julie, a sixteen-year-old girl, expressed it like this: "Having cried myself to sleep many times, I realize the depth of pain a little girl can feel. Now, when I have the opportunity to share my healing with someone else who is struggling, I feel like it was almost worth it. A lot of my friends come to me with their problems, because they say I understand them and can really relate. You know, I think they're right. But it's taken a long time for me to get to the point where I can help anyone."

Children of divorce tend to be more mature and responsible than their peers. Even though their maturity has developed through difficulties, many of the children of divorce that I have spoken with seem to have a wisdom beyond their years. This comes from having to grapple with issues that other kids don't have to face until they are much older—issues like loyalty, betrayal, adultery, child support, court hearings, rejection, and so on. Although you would probably prefer to have your children avoid these issues, they do help the child move from concrete to abstract reasoning.

One teenage boy put it this way: "I used to just think about me and my needs. Now I'm more concerned for my little brother. I've tried to come alongside of him and support him through this mess because I know how much I hurt when I was his age. I sometimes just take him fishing or something, so we can get away and talk. We cry together, laugh together. We're closer now than ever."

Children of divorce must choose either to fight the changes in their life or become more responsible people. Most will eventually stop blaming or looking to others for the solution to their problems and realize that they've got to take responsibility for their own future. Many people don't learn this until they are adults, but the pressure cooker of divorce has a way of maturing a child more quickly than might otherwise be expected.

Margie, a seventeen-year-old, said, "Before the divorce, my life was fairly secure. Everything was taken care of as far as my schooling, my welfare, and even my future were concerned. Then, when everything fell apart, I learned that the world isn't secure at all. While in high school, I had to work, take care of my brothers and sisters, cook, and clean. I feel like I got a taste of motherhood.

"I'm leaving for college soon, and I know that I'm going to have to work my way through, but I know I'll value my education more and not take things for granted as much. After all, it's my education and my future."

This increased level of responsibility may reach to the child's moral development. Children of divorce are faced with their parents' moral failures: lies, manipulations, maybe even cheating and stealing. Obviously this forces the child to think more about what she believes and how she is going to live her life. It is no longer enough to believe something merely because her mother told her so.

After a sometimes rebellious transition, most children of divorce settle down to a belief system that is based on what they have concluded about life, rather than what their parents have taught them. Even though this may be a scary thought to parents, the belief system these children develop is actually more mature and enduring than is one based on the beliefs of the parents. Nancy explained it this way: "All my life my parents taught me right and wrong. Then I saw my mom and dad break just about every one of their own rules. It forced me to really examine what was truth. Today I have a strong faith in God, which helps me in every area of my life."

Children of divorce are better able to put life experiences into a proper perspective. John said, "When you've been through some of the worst things that can happen in life at age eight, everything else that comes your way seems so much easier. You've survived divorce and so now you're determined that nothing else is going to get you down again. I still have difficult times, but I always go back to my parents' divorce and compare it to that. Then I know I'm going to be just fine."

Growing up in a storybook life may leave children with the expectation that they are going to live "happily ever after." It can be a real shocker when they discover that the fairy tale is not true. I have seen adults come apart because they were not prepared for the realities of life, realities that children of divorce learn early. Even though we would rather shield our kids from them, such difficulties have a way of teaching lessons that last a lifetime.

Children of divorce are very motivated to succeed in marriage. Having experienced firsthand the effects of divorce, the children usually become determined that it won't happen to them. Unfortunately, many are still not able to make their marriage work. Even deeper than this determination is the realization that you can't take certain things for granted, such as someone's love.

Having grown up in a happy, secure home environment, it wasn't until after college that I learned that the world isn't always a fair place and that bad things *do* happen to good people. This was a difficult lesson that many of us learned after stumbling into relationships with people we thought were trustworthy and good. Children of divorce learn at a very young age that good people (their parents) can hurt them and perhaps can't always be trusted. When looking for a mate, these children tend to be much more cautious.

This is the positive side of the finding that children of divorce (especially women) tend to delay marriage because of their fear of betrayal. This may be good if it helps them avoid a future divorce by not marrying the first man they fall in love with. In fact there is some preliminary evidence in Judith Wallerstein's longitudinal study that suggests that even though children of divorce are afraid of commitment, they eventually settle into relationships that last. She says, "I'm predicting that after a lot of trial and error, after a lot of getting hurt, a significant number of children of divorce will find a relationship that will stick."

When I interviewed teenagers of divorce for this book, I asked the question, "How do you think your future will be affected, particularly your getting married?" Every one of them responded that they would be cautious about whom they choose to marry. Some indicated they would be looking for particular qualities in a potential mate. One teen girl said, "I don't mean to be picky but I know that I want to know someone for a long time before I marry him. I want to be sure he's not going to change later on. I want a guy who is kind and compassionate, but most important, someone who has a strong faith in God and knows the meaning of commitment."

One parent summarized this point best: "If my divorce helps to keep my daughter from having to go through the same thing someday, then it was worth it!"

Summary

Even though there are probably hundreds of ways in which the child's personality is affected by divorce, there are three that are most commonly cited. A lack of motivation and direction is evident in the lives of approximately 40 percent of the young men whose parents divorced; difficulty in relationships is seen among approximately 66 percent of the young women in one study; an overburdened child syndrome is found in about 15 percent of the adult children of divorce.

While these effects are troubling to read about, there can be positive outcomes from a divorce. The strength of character and resiliency that have been demonstrated by many children of divorce are encouraging and challenging to us all.

As we move into the next section, which deals with helping your child recover in the most healthy way, I think again of the Serenity Prayer. The first part of this classic prayer asks for serenity to "accept the things that I cannot change," but here I'm focusing on the second part—we all need the courage to change the things we can change and need to change.

Part 3

Helping
Your Child

Breaking the News

I was five or six when I first remember my parents fighting a lot. I remember that Dad was working more and more and that I missed him. There were times when Dad was gone for weeks at a time. When we asked my mom where Dad was, she would always say, "Away on a business trip." I now know that my dad and mom were separated. Whenever they tried to reconcile, my mom would say that Dad was home for a vacation. This went on for about two years. It didn't matter what my mom said anymore, my brother and I knew there was

*something wrong and we knew that we didn't like it.
When Mom finally told us the truth, that she and
Dad were getting a divorce, it was only because he
was getting married to someone else and wanted my
brother and me to be in the wedding.*

*I wish my mom had told us the truth two years
earlier. Then we could have started the grieving
process and maybe been more accepting of our new
stepmother and stepsister. That was really tough
for us to swallow.*

—a fourteen-year-old boy

As soon as the possibility of divorce is apparent, you
need to start talking with your kids about it. I know it
may already be too late for you to undo the way you broke
the news to your children, but if you have not told them
yet, do so now. Kids usually know there is something
going on long before you realize they know. They also
understand more than you think.

There is no ideal way to break the news to your children. The story at the beginning of this chapter tells how
not to do it. I want to offer a collection of suggestions
to you as you take on this difficult task. This whole chapter will tend to sound like a cookbook of do's and don'ts.
Keep in mind that it's just a list of guidelines, some of
which you can implement and some of which you can't.
Remember our prayer: "God, grant me the serenity to
accept the things that I cannot change, the courage to
change the things that I can, and the wisdom to know
the difference." Also keep in mind that there are no
secret formulas or even standard methods of operation.
Your child is an individual, and therefore you will need
to tailor this information to fit your situation and your
child.

Speak the Truth in Love

In the Book of Ephesians the apostle Paul writes that we are to "speak the truth in love." This is the best way that I can describe the communication that should take place between all parties involved in a separation or divorce. This may be nearly impossible at times, but I believe that it needs to be our goal. Let's explore how this guideline plays itself out by answering some of the most commonly asked questions I hear from divorcing parents.

When should we tell the kids?

I think it is important to tell the kids what is going on as soon as both of you know, but don't feel compelled to tell the children anything of a personal nature between you and your spouse. If the children are older, then they will know that something is not right and may even know that you are seeing a counselor. If they ask, use this as an opportunity to demonstrate the proper way to handle problems: "Your mother and I are having some personal problems that we need to work out. Because we are committed to each other and to the family, we want to get help in resolving these problems as quickly as we can." If your children are too young to understand the problem, or if they don't ask, then there is no need to try to tell them what is going on.

Once the problem reaches a point where divorce or separation is apparent, then it affects the whole family. The children need to be told as soon as it can be arranged. This should be delayed only if you need to work out some of the details or if the separation happens to fall on an important day, such as Christmas or the birthday of one of the children. It is reasonable to wait to break the news

141

until some of the details are worked out, such as: *Where will Mom live? Where will Dad live? Where will the kids stay? And how often will we see each parent?* You need to present a scenario that is well thought through and reassuring to the children if at all possible. If these matters cannot be settled, and it looks like the children are going to find out, you may need to sit them down and tell them as much as you know.

Many parents try to protect their children from the truth as long as possible. One study found that 80 percent of the preschoolers questioned had received no information about their parents' separation. Parents do a disservice to the child by withholding such information. Withholding merely creates anxiety about the future and distrust of the parent.

How should we tell the kids and how much should we tell them?

If possible, both parents should sit down with the kids and together tell them about the separation or divorce before one of the parents leaves. If the separation happens abruptly, the parent with the children will need to give them some preliminary information right away, but as soon as it can be arranged, both parents need to come together to tell the children what will happen to the family. This method is important for several reasons. First, with both parents present, there is the greatest possibility of a balanced and honest presentation. Second, if the children have any questions, they need to address them to the parent who is best able to answer. And third, the united front makes it clear that both parents are in agreement on the decision. This helps to reduce the splitting of loyalties, the playing of one parent against the other, and the children's fantasy that their parents will work it out. If one parent is missing, the children are likely to think, *Yeah, that's what Mom says, but Dad will have a different story.*

If one parent is not present, then it is even more important that the parent who tells the children be committed to speaking the truth as lovingly as possible. Representing both sides of the issue is very difficult when you are so emotionally involved. Even though you are irate with the other parent, you want to let the children know that it is an issue between the parents and that you both still love them.

If your child has questions about the other parent or his or her reasons for leaving, try to answer the questions as honestly as possible. Don't attribute motives or make judgments about the other parent. Just state as nicely as you can what you know to be true. For example, don't say, "Your father left because he's irresponsible. He's probably going to be moving in with his girlfriend and forget all about us." Try this instead: "Your father loves you very much but doesn't seem to love me. Even though he does not want to live with me anymore, he wants to visit with you whenever he can."

By taking the high road, you will end up better off, even if you have good reason to drag your spouse's reputation through the mud. Remember, the children will know the truth sooner or later, and it would be better for you if they remember you as the one who chose the most loving course.

When deciding how much you should tell the kids, you must take into consideration their developmental level. As one mother put it, "Get the key points across, and then allow for open discussion. If the child knows enough to ask the question, then they're old enough to get an honest answer."

The key points to cover include:

- How did this happen? What are the reasons?
- Do you still love me? Does my mother/father still love me? Am I wanted?
- How will my life be changed? Where will I live, go to school, church?
- Am I part of the reason for the breakup? Could I have done something to avoid this separation/divorce?

It is most important to cover what will happen to the children. Reassure them of your love for them and be prepared to back it up with actions. Give the child permission to love *both* parents. For preschoolers it is important that you reassure them that they will be cared for and then explain the divorce in terms they can understand. For example: "Mommy loves you very much, and Daddy loves you very much. You are going to live with me, and we will stay in this house where you will eat, sleep, and play, just like you do now. Daddy is going to live in an apartment nearby so that he can come and visit you every week. In fact he will pick you up this Saturday and show you where he lives. You will eat lunch there, and then he will bring you back home where I will be waiting to hear all about your day. We are separating because we don't want to fight anymore. We will all be sad about Daddy leaving, but Mommy and Daddy would be even sadder if Daddy stayed here and we fought a lot."

Children who are elementary age or older need more specific information, particularly about where they will live and the visitation arrangements. They will also require more specifics about what went wrong. You need to be as honest as you can, without discussing anything about sexual problems. If possible, avoid placing blame, since it is true that divorce is rarely, if ever, all one person's fault.

Don't expect your children to understand your explanations or to ask all of their questions the first time you talk about it. Be prepared to explain the situation and answer questions over and over again. Stress that the decision to separate or divorce is an adult decision. It was not their fault, nor can they do anything to get their parents back together. (See suggested books for children in the appendix under Children's Books.)

What if the truth is particularly ugly or hard to talk about?

You need to tell the truth in as loving a way as you can. It may not be as difficult as you imagine. The earlier your kids hear the truth, the sooner they can start to deal with the problem and begin the healing process. You need to use discretion, considering the age of the child and how much they can understand, but once again, if they are old enough to ask the question, they are old enough to hear an honest answer.

For example, if Dad is leaving because he has a girlfriend or he is a homosexual, you may not want to give them all of this information in the first meeting. Soon thereafter, however, you need to tell them what is really going on. Sooner or later, the kids hear the whispers and innuendos, so it is best that they hear it in a straightforward manner from their parents. If possible, the information should come from the parent with "the problem" (that is, the one whose behavior/lifestyle is prompting the breakup). In that way the children know that they are hearing firsthand information, which is usually more reliable. Then they have the opportunity to openly discuss their questions and concerns.

If that parent is not available, or not willing to talk with the children, then it obviously falls on the other parent to present as balanced an explanation as possible. Then, if they have questions, the custodial parent may want to offer to let them discuss the issue with someone a little more neutral. This may be an aunt or uncle they trust, a counselor at the school or the church, or a relative of the departing spouse— anyone the children may view as being more objective. The children may not want to talk with someone else, but it is important that at least the offer is made. This allows them the opportunity to seek a "second opinion" without feeling that they are betraying the custodial parent.

This open communication is one of the key elements in a healthy family. Dysfunctional families are marked by too much interaction, known as enmeshment, too little communication or emotional distancing, and distorted messages, as found in controlling and manipulative families. Healthy interactions allow for open discussion and honest questioning. Good communication also invites verification, so that everyone is sure to have a balanced view of the matter.

What about cases where the child is actually abandoned by one of his parents?

When someone apparently abandons his or her children, it is difficult to speak the truth in a loving way. This is not only because it is hard to be loving in these situations, but because you rarely know what the truth is. I don't believe that you can tell the child, "Daddy doesn't love you" or "Daddy's not coming back," because probably neither statement is true. Many parents, both mothers and fathers, who apparently abandon their children will later try to contact them and reestablish a relationship. In addition, the fact that the parent left does not prove his or her lack of love. Studies have shown that many times the leaving parents feel so bad about themselves that they believe the most loving thing to do is to get out of their family's life. Their thinking can be so distorted that they feel like the best thing for everyone is that they disappear for a time.

Therefore, in cases of abandonment, the remaining parent needs to balance the explanatory comments so that the children do not have undue hope *or* despair. "I don't know if your father is coming back or not. We need to go on with our lives as if he won't be back, but you never know; someday he may realize what he is missing and decide to come back to see you."

Another critical reassurance is the child's lovability. "I don't know if your father loves you or not, but I do know that you are a very lovable child. He is not thinking properly right now and has to work through some problems, but I know that if he ever works through those problems, he will realize what a wonderful child you are." Or, "I know your father loves you. He just is not able to express it or show it right now because he is trying to figure out his own life. That does not change the fact that you are a wonderful and lovable child. Your father's problems have nothing to do with you."

Aren't children really tougher than we think? In other words, can't they eventually recover, no matter how difficult the truth is to hear?

Yes, most children are more resilient than we think. But that does not mean we should tell them everything. Unfortunately this idea of resiliency has often been misinterpreted to mean, "Children are more mature than you think." As a result, children are often expected to handle the impact of divorce or other devastating news with passive serenity. Kids are tougher than we think in their ability to handle reality when their parents take the time to communicate honestly with them. *Details are seldom necessary, but honesty is critical.*

It is important to remember that one of the casualties of divorce is trust. Trust is destroyed when parents who once said, "We'll always be here for you," are now telling you that Mommy or Daddy will be living elsewhere. The only way to rebuild your child's trust is through honesty and open communication.

If the truth is too much to handle, your child may withdraw or react hysterically. It is natural for parents to back off a bit at that time, and this is probably best. But don't back away from the truth or indicate that the family might get back together, just to relieve the tension. Eventually you need to encourage your child to express his feelings, to let it all out. It takes great courage on the part of parents to try to understand their children's feelings and allow them to express their pain. However, this will accelerate acceptance and growth on the part of the child. Further, parents who make the effort to understand and comfort their children usually find that they themselves are comforted.

How can I expect my children to react when we give them the news?

Your children's reactions will vary according to their developmental level and their personality, but generally you can expect some of the following reactions.

- *An underreaction.* This may be a form of denial and the beginning of the grieving process as described in chapter 4. Don't be surprised when your child reacts with, "Can I go out and play now?"

- *A preoccupation with egocentric thoughts.* For all the reasons described in chapter 2, your child may react with, "What about my birthday?" or, "Who's going to take me to Disney World?" These are merely concrete expressions of his fear for the future.
- *A lack of interest in the details of the divorce.* This reaction may reflect the child's inability to comprehend the news and the fear of talking about it. When you ask if your child has questions, it is not unusual for the child to express none at the time. Therefore, it is important that you follow up your initial discussion with other opportunities for the child to express his concerns.

Whatever your children's reactions, it is critical that you continually reassure them, through every stage of their development, that they are loved by both parents and that the divorce was not their fault. Explaining the separation or divorce to your children cannot really be done in one session. It will require new explanations and reassurances as the children grow and mature. Even in adulthood, your children will still have lingering questions that need to be answered. If you communicate well, you will create an atmosphere for them that encourages their inquiries throughout life.

What if we've already told the children, but we did it all wrong?

I don't believe it's ever too late to go back and do it right. Granted, some of the questions have already been answered or figured out by the kids, but that doesn't mean that it wouldn't help to have an open discussion about how they feel about all of the changes. You may think that none of these things are an issue for your kids, because they've never mentioned them. That may be because you've never given your kids permission to talk about these issues by opening the conversation.

If you've done it "all wrong" by giving the children distorted, biased, or unloving information about the other parent, then I believe it is best to admit your wrongs to the children, ask for their forgiveness, correct the wrongs, and then vow to be more objective and positive in the future.

If possible, and this might really be asking a lot, contact your former spouse to see if he or she would be willing to have a joint meeting with the children. This could go a long way toward establishing a respectful, cooperative effort in co-parenting the children, which benefits everyone.

Summary

Let me reiterate the most important points regarding the parents' communication with their children:

1. Be honest and open in the way you present the information. Give explanations, not defenses or opinions.
2. Focus on what will happen to each child. Assure each child of his continued well-being, in spite of difficult transitions.
3. Make sure the children understand that they were not the cause of the divorce.
4. Give clear and definite statements of mutual love and acceptance. Be prepared to back them up through hugs, showing interest in their world, and a listening ear.

5. Let them know that they can't get their parents back together. Encourage a realistic view of what life will be like after the divorce.
6. Expect that you will have to reinforce this information by opening discussions with your children about the divorce at regular intervals throughout their lives.

Restructuring the Family

My whole world was turned upside down *when my parents broke up. My mom took my brother and me away from our home to live with our grandparents for a few months. After that we moved into this lousy apartment with no furniture. I had to attend a school that I used to make fun of. They were our rivals in sports, and the kids all seemed like druggies. Now I'm in this school, trying to make friends. It's like my worst nightmare come true.*

My parents are always arguing about stupid stuff, mostly money and when my brother and I are coming over to see Dad. I get tired of being in the middle of it. My mom tells me to ask Dad for the support check when I see him. Then my dad starts yelling at me about how he'd send the check if "your mother would let me see you guys when she's supposed to!"

I hate it when my parents talk to each other, because they always fight. But when they're not talking, I end up having to send messages back and forth.

—a sixteen-year-old boy

Restructuring a home and a family is always difficult and stressful. When you add the grief and trauma of a divorce, you have the makings of an explosive situation. The purpose of this chapter is to provide guidelines as to how to make these changes with the least turmoil and emotional harm to all the participants. Granted, we can never eliminate all of the negative consequences or make up for our mistakes, but there is much that we as parents can do to smooth the transition.

Here are some of the more prevalent problem areas in the transition from married life to single parenting.

Custody and Visitation

Other than money issues, I'm sure there is no other issue that is more troublesome or emotionally charged than the custody and visitation rights of each parent. I will not discuss the different types of arrangements and how well they work, because there are too many variables involved. For information on your options, I encourage you to talk with a lawyer or a divorce mediation specialist. Each state has its own laws as well as trends, which vary according to the views of the judges who oversee such cases. You need to be advised by someone who is familiar with the system and the way it works in your area.

However, as a psychologist, I can address the emotional side of the custody and visitation battle. First, don't make it a battle. Remember, the more you can resolve amicably between yourselves, the more you will save in money, time, wear and tear on your nerves, and damaging effects to your children. I can't tell you how many times I have heard stories like Lori's: "My husband and I fought over who would get the children for almost five years. It started out bad, but only got worse with each new round of hearings. By the time we were done, we had used every possible devious tactic and called each other every name in the book. Of course, the children heard it all, and the only winners were the lawyers. Our legal fees were over forty thousand dollars, which was more than we had tried to split between us some five years earlier."

Whenever divorcing parents tell me that they want to fight the other parent and come out on top, I feel compelled to tell them that *there are no winners in a divorce,* except perhaps the lawyers. If you think that you are going to fight your particular case until you finally win, please rethink what you are doing. You are not going to win. You will merely run out of resources and energy, at which point you will compromise to a position you probably could have obtained much earlier at half the expense.

Now that I have made an absolute statement, let me give you the exception. In cases of abuse or extreme misconduct on the part of the other parent, you need to fight for the rights of your children. Standing up for your own rights is something that I encourage all parents to do, but it is not worth battling the other parent, unless you or your children are in some type of physical or emotional danger. Fortunately this is the exception rather than the rule.

Since you are not the most objective person to judge whether or not your case falls into the "extreme" category, I encourage you to seek third-party objectivity from a counselor or spiritual advisor. You need to recognize that your friends and relatives are usually biased in your favor, and your lawyer may tend to advocate an adversarial position for obvious reasons.

Here are some other guidelines in regard to custody and visitation rights.

Set up a good, workable visitation arrangement as soon as the separation occurs. This will help the children adjust to a new routine, while assuring continuity with both parents. This also paves the way for a smoother settlement of the "official agreement." Keep the visitation consistent so that children know what to expect and when they will see the other parent. When unscheduled changes occur, let your children know as soon as possible.

With teenagers, flexibility is needed because of their busy schedules and outside activities. Both parents should respect the teen's wishes, but not at the expense of the relationship with the other parent. For example, if your teen is planning to work on weekends, this must be decided and arranged in consultation with both parents, since it tends to greatly affect the relationship with the noncustodial parent.

Holidays need to be planned well in advance and then explained to the children. Don't wait until the week before Christmas to talk with the other parent about how the holiday is to be handled. This leads to undue stress for the parents and the child at a time when you need it the least. Older children and teens may be consulted as to their wishes for the holidays, but once again the final decision must be the parents'.

Unless your children are preschoolers, you should consult with them about the visitation arrangement. This is particularly true of teenagers. Even though you ask them their opinion, make sure they understand that the final decision is up to the parents and will not be decided by the children. Keep in mind your child's tendency to tell you what she thinks you want to hear. Therefore, you should expect that she will say one thing to you and something else to the other parent. Don't embarrass your child or punish her for this. She wants desperately the love and loyalty of both parents. Use her wishes as input into your final decision.

If a court case becomes inevitable, try to keep the children out of it. If their testimony is crucial, see if it can be handled in the judge's chambers, through a court appointed psychologist, or via videotape. Don't force a courtroom confrontation that will compel the children to testify for or against one of their parents.

Keep the communication lines open between you and the other parent. Keep all discussions of changes in the arrangements and any money issues between the two of you. Don't pass messages through the children. Try to have these discussions over the phone when the kids are not around. That way, if they become unavoidably heated, your children will not get emotionally involved in the disagreement. Don't wait until the other parent comes to pick up or drop off the children to say, "Oh, by the way . . ." As you know, this leads to disagreements, which the children can't help but witness. (If you have a particularly amicable relationship, you may have no problem with last-minute changes.)

When the children are back with you, encourage them to talk about their time with the other parent, unless you find that you cannot listen without reacting negatively. Don't pump them for specific information, such as dating relationships or how your ex-spouse is choosing to spend money. You know the motivation behind these questions and you also know what that does to you. Ask, "Did you guys have fun with your father (or mother) this weekend?" Then be prepared to bite your tongue when they talk about how much fun it was or even how nice the new "significant other" is. This is extremely difficult for you but, for the sake of your children, encourage their honest expression of this important part of their life.

If you find that you cannot listen to this information without reacting badly, then be honest enough with your children to say, "It hurts me to hear this right now. I want you to have fun with your dad, and maybe someday we will be able to talk all about it, but for right now maybe we shouldn't." Then find ways to work on your own adjustment so that you can later encourage your children to share with you all areas of their lives, especially their relationship with the other parent, and perhaps a stepparent.

Both parents should set aside time alone with each child. This gives them the opportunity to create special bonds and to talk on a deeper level than is possible when all the children are together. This has proven to be an important factor in the building of a strong sense of security and a healthy self-image.

Avoid being a "Disneyland Daddy" or a "Magic Mountain Mommy." Parents who do not normally live with the children tend to avoid the normal patterns of a realistic home environment. They want to make sure the children have a good time when they come to visit, so they may eat out frequently, do special things every visit, and fudge on the rules regarding such things as bedtime and homework. To decrease the instability and competition between the parents, they should strive to provide the same stable and consistent discipline that is expected by the custodial parent. Although special events are nice, the majority of the time should be part of a daily routine, similar to what they do in the other home. Avoid presents or treats that seem like relationship bribes. Focus on building the relationship with your children through open communication and time spent doing everyday tasks.

Each child needs to feel the continued love of both parents. The children must also feel that each parent encourages their relationship with the other parent. Ready access to the noncustodial parent, by phone and in person, is necessary. *You* will benefit if you help your child accept and love the other parent, even when the other parent doesn't do the same.

Child Support and Alimony

You need to discuss with your lawyer or mediator how much alimony and/or child support you should receive. My concern here is how these payments (actually, the lack of these payments) affect your children. The rule is that all fathers (we're assuming here that Dad is the noncustodial parent) make their child-support and/or alimony payment on time. In reality, however, we know that not all payments are on time and that many fathers make no payments at all. Whenever this occurs, the children are inevitably affected.

Unless the father is unemployed or on the verge of bankruptcy, his resistance to keeping his financial obligation is usually the result of unresolved anger or resentment toward the mother. Even though the father swears he loves his children, he may resist fulfilling his obligation to them to make a point. Unfortunately this causes the children to suffer. Not only are the financial needs of the children being neglected, but the father is contributing to an unpleasant atmosphere for the children at home. Their mother is placed under undue financial strain and inevitably will have to tell the children things like, "I'm sorry I can't get you those sneakers; your father hasn't sent the support check." So what have you gained by withholding your payment, and whom have you really punished?

Many times withholding payments is the result of a conflict over visitation arrangements. Fathers tell me that they are not going to pay because their former spouse does not send the children when she is supposed to. Predictably, the mother then tells me that she doesn't send the kids on time because of the father's sporadic payments. This never-ending Catch-22 has no winners, and the children end up suffering the most. For the sake of your children, *don't do it!*

Child support and alimony are legal obligations and have nothing to do with your children. You need to keep your obligations regardless of your relationship with your children or your former spouse. If you are not happy with the arrangement, then take it up *privately* with the other parent. If that does not resolve your concerns, then take it to your lawyer or mediator. Don't resort to punishing your children for your inability to get along with their mother.

On the other hand, I'm not going to let the moms off so easily. Just because your former spouse doesn't make payments on time or doesn't make them at all, you have no right to block his relationship with his children. The same principles apply. The father's visitation rights are a legal obligation and are critical to your child's healthy adjustment to divorce (assuming the parent is not abusive). Therefore, his nonpayment must be taken up with him first, and then taken to the legal authorities. Fortunately the courts are beginning to take these matters more seriously and have started cracking down on "deadbeat dads." Many, however, continue to fall through the cracks in the system.

But what do we tell the children? In the beginning, as little as possible. Children, and even teens, should be kept out of the financial arrangements and disagreements. However, when the problem persists, such as when no payment has been made in several months, then you may have to tell the children the truth. Let them know that you don't want them to get involved in the dispute, but because their father has not made several payments, you will all have to tighten your belts a bit. Let them know that you want them to continue having a good relationship with their father. Discourage them from trying to scold him or "punish" him with bad behavior when they see him. Assure them that you will work out the problem on your own.

I know that this advice is hard to swallow when you're in the midst of the financial crisis or when you can't begin to see any redeeming qualities in the other parent. So let me remind you of the long-term effects of divorce on children and once again point out that a continued relationship with both parents is crucial to the psychological well-being of your children. Try to determine and focus on the underlying issue in the dispute and how you can resolve it without putting your children in the middle.

Your Child and the School

Mrs. Graham didn't want the school to find out that her husband had left. With her two children, Martha and Michael, in a private Christian school, she was afraid that the school's conservative philosophy would prejudice the teachers and administrators against her children. If the teachers knew, she reasoned, they would watch her children too closely and look for trouble.

The problem with Mrs. Graham's cautious attitude is that her fears are probably unfounded and she may be depriving the children of significant help. As a school psychologist in Philadelphia, I consulted with teachers and principals in more than twenty public and private schools. I found that teachers were sensitive and compassionate when they became aware of a student's struggles. They were harder on children when they started falling behind or missing assignments with no apparent reason. But in the case of divorce, teachers would make allowances for the child's distractibility, academic regression, emotional withdrawal, or hostility.

Teachers have access to a variety of resources to help children. Books, tapes, videos, and counselors are usually available for your children, as long as the school is aware of your need. The school may be holding support groups for children of divorce or may be able to refer you to group meetings that are held in your community. But you won't know this unless you inform the school of what is going on at home.

Teenagers usually have a number of teachers, and at that age your kids probably wouldn't appreciate it if you contacted all the teachers to explain the problems at home. But a call to your child's guidance counselor or advisor might be helpful. If it is a large school, the counselor will probably do little, unless there's a special program available or your child comes in for help. Older children are more influenced by their peer group, and therefore will tend to talk with friends far more than they will talk with teachers or a counselor. Encourage the peer interaction, especially with other children who have been through the same thing. They can be a tremendous help to each other. (This is a major premise of Fresh Start's "Kids in the Middle" program: kids helping other kids.) However, you may need to correct distorted peer feedback from time to time, especially if your child's friends are immature or hostile. Try to be aware of the kind of support your child is receiving from other kids.

Changes at Home

"When my family got a divorce, my whole world changed forever. We moved to a new home, a new school district, a new church, and all new friends. I don't know what hurt the most, missing my dad or missing my friends from my old neighborhood and school."

This quote from an eleven-year-old girl illustrates the child's need for stability amid the turmoil. There will always be changes to face. Some of these changes may even be good, especially over the long term. Yet when separation or divorce first occurs, try to keep the changes to a minimum. If you have to move, try to stay in the same school district, or close to it, where your children can still connect with the same social group.

Your own friendships will probably evolve toward more single people and fewer married couples. As parents get together in singles groups and social clubs, it is inevitable that the children will socialize as well. This can result in positive new relationships with other kids who have been through similar life changes. This reinforces your children's realization that they are not alone and gives them the opportunity to talk to other kids about their concerns. Nevertheless, as a parent, you can't push these new friendships too quickly. Encourage the child to continue her long-term friendships, while allowing new relationships to develop naturally.

Keep the household schedule, responsibilities, and discipline as consistent as possible. If you did not work outside the home before, and now you have to, your schedule will obviously change. Sit down with your children, explain the need for the changes, and then let them know what they can expect for the future. It is most important that your children know that you want to be with them, that you want to care for them, but that the changes force everyone to take on more responsibilities. For example, you may need to say, "I have to go back to work to help pay the bills. This means that I won't be here when you get home from school. I would love to be here for you, fix your snack, and hear all about your day. But, unfortunately, you'll have to wait until I get home at 5:30. That means you'll have to fix your own snack and you may even need to help set the table before I get home. What's important is that we work together and make our relationship even stronger than it was before."

Here are a few additional guidelines that should help you handle the changes at home.

Although increased responsibilities are inevitable, don't allow your kids to become hyperresponsible, taking on burdens and chores that they should not shoulder. Let your children remain children. No matter how mature they act, don't fool yourself into believing they can take on adult responsibilities. Boys are particularly susceptible to thinking, *Now that I'm the man of the house, I need to be here for Mom.* One boy told me that he could not go away to school in the fall because his mom was going through a difficult time and would need a man around the house. Remember the overburdened child syndrome.

It is important that parents avoid confiding in their children as if they were peers. This can happen when moms talk to their daughters about "what a tough life it is out there." Or when Dad tells his son all about the women he's dating. Let your child remain a child.

As a parent, you want a close relationship with your children, but there must be some boundaries in that relationship. If you have a problem with setting limits and boundaries in relationships or grew up in a home where boundaries were confused, then you may be unconsciously passing this on to your children. If this is the case, I encourage you to seek counseling for your own issues, so that you can create a healthier balance for your children.

Don't force your children to make choices that will create loyalty conflicts for them. For example, don't ask your children, "Who do you want to spend your birthday with, your mom or your dad?" This creates a no-win situation for your children. If they pick you, they hurt the other parent. And how can they tell you that they'd rather be with the other parent? It would be best to get their input by asking a neutral question like, "How would you like to spend the holiday?" If they neglect the other parent, you may want to suggest a compromise that includes both parents. This approach demonstrates that you are sincere in your desire that they have a good relationship with the other parent and discourages your children's tendency to tell you what they think you want to hear.

Encourage your children to keep their fond memories of the other parent. Many times, after a divorce, parents do a clean sweep of the house, throwing away all pictures or mementos that remind them of the other parent. While I understand the feelings behind this, try to save a photo album or two for your children to remind them of good family times together. A special picture or memento beside their bed or in a wallet is also recommended. Remember, if you suggest it, this gives the child permission to love the other parent. If you don't suggest it, your child may assume, *Mom would hit the roof if she saw a picture of* him *around.*

Special Friends and Stepparents

When a parent is trying to restructure his or her family, adding a new friend or a stepparent to the mix is like throwing a monkey wrench into the works. New relationships generally cause a whole new set of adjustments that take years to work through. If, within the first two years, these are added to the children's adjustment to the trauma of divorce, all of the emotions will be intensified, and acceptance can be much further away. Therefore, many therapists recommend that newly divorced people not get involved in intimate relationships for at least two years following their divorce. This helps not only you but your children make adjustments to the divorce.

This does not mean that you should avoid new friendships, or even relationships with the opposite sex. On the contrary, these friendships, assuming they are healthy, are vital to your recovery. But you do need to avoid *committed* relationships with the opposite sex and emotional entanglements that complicate the recovery process for you and your children. These "rebound relationships" rarely last and most often lead to more pain for everybody involved. The statistics on remarriage show that when people remarry within two years of their divorce, they have a greater than 80 percent chance of going through another divorce. Do you or your children need that? For those who wait for two years, however, the odds of a successful remarriage increase to about 50 percent, which is the same percentage as for first-time marriages.

Unfortunately the reality is that your divorce was probably precipitated by the involvement of another person in your life or the life of your spouse and perhaps both. So now what do you do? Many parents will use the existence of an extramarital affair as an excuse to keep the children away from the other parent. While I do not condone the extramarital relationship and understand the depth of the other parent's resentment and hurt, once again I must defer to the greater good of the children. As one "kid in the middle" put it: "My dad left my mom to live with his girlfriend. When Dad asked if he could pick us up for a visit, my mom refused to let us go over, because she didn't agree with his lifestyle. We knew that what my dad had done was wrong, and in many ways we were really ticked at him. But he was still our father, and we still loved him. Mom not letting us go only created a bunch of mudslinging between my parents. I think I would have respected my mom a lot more if she had told us how she felt and then allowed us to see him. Now my dad is married to his girlfriend, and our relationship is still strained. I don't want to do it, but sometimes I blame my mom for the fact that I don't really have a relationship with my dad."

Unfortunately dating relationships have a way of becoming an additional battleground in the post-divorce experience. Besides being used as an excuse for curtailing visitation, other pitfalls exist for your children as you become involved in a special relationship. Here are a few additional guidelines as you seek to include opposite-sex relationships in your restructured family.

As the noncustodial parent, it would be best if you curtailed your dating on weekends when your children visit. Parenting needs to be your first priority. Especially in the first few years of your restructured family, you need to give your children as much of your time as possible. Your children will generally view your dates as an intrusion. As one particular person becomes important to you, introduce that person into your children's lives in a very gradual, nonthreatening way.

It is probably much harder for the custodial parent to have a social life. Some potential dates may be scared off by your children, and then there is the problem of the time and energy that it takes to maintain a social life. However, when the opportunity arises, you should not feel guilty about getting a baby-sitter and enjoying a night out. A balance is needed between your right to privacy and your need to be honest with the kids. Your children don't need to meet and approve of everyone you go out with, but you should not hide the fact that you are dating. Your children's trust in you is built when you are honest with them, even though they may not like seeing you go out without them. Expect some acting out and jealous demands on your time and attention.

Don't encourage your casual dates to get close to your children. A positive male role model is *not* a series of men that you happen to date. (And the same can be said for "mother figures" a father might date.) This only confuses your children and reinforces the perception that relationships are not permanent. It adds to their insecurity. While teens are more understanding of temporary relationships, they too are not helped by your pushing your new relationships on them. Integrate your opposite-sex friends into your children's lives only as they become an important part of yours. Then allow the relationship with the children to develop at its own pace, never pushing your children into an artificial acceptance.

Avoid the temptation to ask your children about the other parent's new friends. This makes your children spies and creates additional loyalty conflicts. If they volunteer the information, try to show little reaction. Encourage your children to treat your dates and your ex-spouse's dates with respect. Don't allow the dating relationship to become a source of conflict.

If your children ask you questions about your dating relationships, give them honest answers without personal details. For example, "Do you love so-and-so?" should be answered as honestly as you can without giving information about the depth of your relationship, or your plans for the future. That should wait until you are ready to take definite steps.

If your child asks, "Do you and so-and-so kiss?" you should answer honestly without making a big deal out of it. Give no further details, however, about your physical relationship.

Remarriage

Once a relationship progresses to the point where it looks as if a remarriage is imminent, you need to have a discussion with your children similar to the one described in chapter 8 when you were contemplating separation or divorce. Out of courtesy to your former mate, you may want to forewarn him or her before you tell the kids, so that your ex-spouse can begin to prepare emotionally. Let's face it: Remarriage of either spouse is a difficult transition for both the children and the parents.

Psychologically speaking, this is a big hurdle for the children. It is one that (1) ends the fantasy that their parents might get back together, (2) triggers the fear that the new spouse will take away the love their parent has for them, and (3) creates anxiety about whether or not they will get along with this "intruder" in the family. For the parent getting married, it finally closes one chapter in life and opens the door to new challenges and opportunities. For the parent remaining single, there is the feeling of being left behind and possibly the anxiety of wondering, *Will I ever be able to move on like that?*

As everyone makes the necessary adjustments, the anxiety that grips your children more and more is the feeling, *Now that Dad has a new wife, he will have even less love and less time for me.* This can be particularly threatening if the new marriage includes children. The blending of families is filled with so many complexities that it needs to be the subject of another book. For our purposes, a general review is in order.

Blended Families

In the 1990s roughly one-third of all children spent at least some time with a stepparent before their eighteenth birthday. The blended family is becoming the most common type of family in the United States. And researchers estimate that it takes an average of five years to successfully blend a family. If you're getting remarried now, it's likely that your teenage children will be out of the house before the necessary adjustments are made.

I have two close friends who were both single parents of teenagers. Both were also enjoying new long-term relationships that were moving toward marriage. But rather than go through the difficulties of blending a family, both couples decided to wait until the children were out of the house before they married. I'm not saying that you should do the same; I merely want to point out that the blending of families is more difficult than most people realize. One of these friends explained his decision this way: "I know of more than twenty remarried couples, all with teenagers in their blended families. I can't name one family who hasn't had major difficulties with their children after the marriage. I just decided that I didn't want to do that to my kids, so I've postponed my own remarriage for another two years. By then my youngest will leave for college."

A mother of a blended family described the following interaction between her teenage son and her new husband. "Before I married Jim, he and my son, Paul, were like best friends. I was so excited because I thought that now, after thirteen years of being by ourselves, Paul was going to have a father figure. The strangest thing happened though. As soon as we got back from the honeymoon, I noticed my son acting a little strange around Jim. Within a few weeks they were barely speaking, and now, after three years of marriage, Paul and Jim can't even look at each other without getting in a fight. I don't know what happened when Jim and I married, but something obviously clicked off for my son."

This example is not unlike many of the stories that I have heard from stepparents who are horrified by what happens when they try to blend a family. It never seems to be easy, and the way everyone gets along before the wedding does not seem to be a very good indication of what to expect after the wedding. In fact it is not at all unusual for the children to push you toward marrying so-and-so and then cause havoc after the wedding, saying they never really liked old so-and-so.

If you are thinking about a remarriage, I recommend getting a book that deals specifically with remarriage and stepparenting issues. (See suggested books in the appendix under Remarriage.) For a general review of some of the issues you will face, here are a few guidelines.

The potential stepparent needs to get to know the children in a gradual and natural way. In the beginning, fun outings are best because they reduce the tension of making conversation. Once the initial transitions are over, however, normal family activities are best.

Don't expect instant rapport between your children and the new stepparent. These relationships take time, usually many years. If the relationship seems to go well from the beginning, expect a strained transition later.

Younger children usually adjust more quickly to a stepparent than do older children and teenagers.

The stepparent should try to observe the family customs and traditions. This includes the giving of gifts to the children on special occasions, the way holidays are celebrated, even making every Friday night "pizza night." But be careful not to overdo the gift giving, since children will tend to view this as a bribe.

Don't push your children to participate in your wedding. They may feel intense pressure to be loyal to the other parent. Let them know of your plans, and tell them that you would like for them to take part but that you will let them decide for themselves. Then give them several weeks, if possible, to decide.

If the new stepparent does not have children, he or she needs to learn about child development and parenting. Don't assume parenting will come naturally. This person is taking on a big commitment, practically overnight, and needs to prepare thoroughly.

Don't expect your children to love or respect their stepparent as much as they do their biological parent. It's unrealistic to expect this and sets the stepparent up for tremendous disappointment.

Don't force your children to call the new stepparent Mom or Dad. Find out what they would prefer to call the stepparent, and then try to compromise on a name or nickname that is acceptable to everyone, including your former spouse. (Yes, even after your remarriage, the lines of communication with your ex-spouse need to stay open.)

Continue to spend individual time with each of your children and constantly remind them of your undiminished love for them. Keep in mind the child's expectation that with each new adult or child in your life, you will have less love for her. This is particularly strong if there is a stepchild about the same age as your own child or if there is a new baby born into the blended family.

While your children need to respect and listen to your new spouse, you need to remain their primary disciplinarian. Young children can take correction from their stepparent rather easily. But older children and teenagers will resist the new authority figure in the home. Therefore it is unfair and unwise to expect the stepparent to take on a major disciplinary role.

Children generally try to play one parent against the other, but this is particularly intense in a stepparent relationship. Try not to get sucked into this divide-and-conquer strategy. When forced into a spouse-or-child dilemma, avoid taking sides right away. Instead, discuss the matter privately with your spouse and then come back and tell the children your decision. Be careful not to undermine your spouse's authority, but be sure to communicate your love for your kids. And, remember, your children will take any kind of discipline best if it comes from you, their biological parent.

Keep in mind that intense feelings of anger and resentment are normal in the blended family, especially among teenagers. Try not to personalize the anger and respond in kind. You are probably bearing the brunt of years of the child's perceived betrayal and disappointment. Be as patient and compassionate as you can be, knowing that this is a very difficult transition for everyone—a transition that, according to statistics, will probably last five years.

Your Children's Stepparent

If your former spouse is remarrying, you will also have adjustments to make—adjustments in your own attitudes and with your children as they report to you their feelings toward the new person in their lives. It is probably a no-win situation for you. If they love their new stepparent, you will feel "replaced." If they don't like their new stepparent, your kids will be troubled, and you'll have to hear weekly complaints.

Here are a few guidelines intended to help you and your children cope with these changes.

If you can't be accepting of your former spouse's remarriage, at least try to stay as neutral and emotionally uninvolved as possible. If you are really struggling with the whole issue, you probably need to talk with a counselor or advisor about your feelings. It will affect your children's adjustment if you continue to have strong negative feelings about these changes.

Give your children permission to attend or participate in the wedding. Forbidding them will only hurt their relationship with *you* in the long run.

As hard as it may be for you to accept, you need to have at least a casual relationship with your former mate's new spouse. You will probably need to talk with him or her on the phone from time to time, and it really doesn't help the children if they see you snarling at each other every time you speak.

Give your children permission to talk about their times at the other parent's house. Listen to their stories about the stepparent and his or her children, but try not to make any judgments or offer your opinion. Try to remain detached when your children complain about or praise the stepparent. Stay out of what goes on in the other household, unless you have good reason for significant concern, such as, "They don't feed us over there!" Then don't assume that it's true. Try to take it up calmly with your former spouse. Involve the stepparent only if you find that you get along better with him or her than you do with your ex-spouse.

Summary

There will always be areas of contention for divorced parents and their children. Here's a brief summary of the guidelines in this chapter for helping your children over some of these difficult hurdles.

Increases Impact of Divorce	Lessens Impact of Divorce
Children are involved in visitation and custody squabbles.	Parents work out custody and visitation arrangement cooperatively.

Children are asked to choose between the parents.	Parents help children avoid loyalty conflicts by encouraging the relationship with the other parent.
Parents use the children to send messages.	Parents keep open the lines of communication with each other.
Parents become too busy or distracted to pay attention to their children.	Parents spend quality time with each child.
Parents use the children and money as leverage to get what they want.	Parents keep money issues separate and away from the children.
Parents isolate themselves and their children.	Parents seek resources and support from a variety of settings, including church, school, family.
Parents expect the children to take the place of the missing parent.	The child remains a child, even though increased responsibilities may be necessary.
Parents deny feelings and do not facilitate discussions with the children.	Parents allow children to grieve.
Parents push children into relationships with a series of the parents' dating partners.	Parents provide for their children stable adult relationships with relatives and family friends.
A remarriage takes place before the children have had time to adjust to the divorce.	At least two years of adjustment pass before a potential stepparent is brought into the children's lives.
Parents maintain angry, bitter feelings.	Parents recover and move on in a healthy new lifestyle.

Parents speak negatively about the other parent in front of the children.	Parents show and express respect for one another.
The absent parent loses contact with the children.	The absent parent maintains consistent contact with the children.

ten

Single Parenting

As a single parent *of two preschool boys, I found my life going through an overwhelming set of changes. At first, I was too depressed to be of any good to anyone, including my boys. But as I moved along, I became determined that I was going to overcome my circumstances. That led me into my "superwoman" role, when I tried to do everything by myself. I took a full-time job, arranged day care for the boys, ran the home, and tried to maintain a social life. I wanted to take the place of their missing father, but what I found was that I was becoming more and more frustrated, and the boys were usually mad at me. What a terrible feeling!*

*Now I'm just trying to be a decent mother. I no
longer need to be superwoman. I don't even have to
be good. I'm settling for doing the best I can and
spending whatever time I can with the boys. It's
like I wanted 100 percent before, and now I'm
settling for 75 percent. But at least I might
preserve my sanity this way, and, who knows,
maybe I'll even enjoy a few days.*
　　　　　　—a thirty-two-year-old single mother

Even though the preceding quote seems a little gloomy,
it is a fairly accurate portrayal of how most single parents
feel at least some time in their lives. There is a sense of
being overwhelmed and having nothing to look forward
to. There is no question that parenting as a single person
is an extremely challenging task, especially if you have
little or no support from the other parent. Yet I know of
many single parents who not only make it on their own
but appear to be happy and fulfilled, raising children who
are very well adjusted.

In this chapter we will look at ways to help you become
more effective as a single parent—not only at raising your
children but also at enjoying the life that you have. I want
to focus on two keys for successful single parenting:

- the way you raise your children
- your own attitude toward your circumstances

Keys to Parenting as a Single Person

An entire book could be written on how to parent as a
single person. (In fact I've written one—*A Fresh Start for
Single Parents*. See appendix under Parenting.) In this

chapter I will present only an overview of single-parenting issues, along with a list of other resources that may be helpful to you if you would like to look more closely at a particular parenting skill.

Single parenting is not a whole lot different from parenting in general. All parenting requires loving discipline, guidance, modeling, nurturing, teaching, and a full range of emotional support. The greatest differences are twofold: Your children tend to be more emotionally needy because of their sense of loss, and you don't have the additional support of a second parent who can share your decisions and frustrations. Therefore, you need to focus on a few critical skills that you can commit yourself to work on. Here are some of the most critical areas.

Provide a Loving Environment

Everyone agrees that a loving environment is one of the most important gifts you can give your children. However, many would disagree as to what a loving environment looks like. Should we be firm or compassionate, foster independence or reliance on the family, give in to our children's wishes or force them to do without? These are all questions that probably have different answers depending on the circumstances and the personality of your child. Regardless of how you handle these concerns, it is essential that you assure your children of your unconditional love for them.

Unconditional love for a child of divorce must come in the form of constant reassurance of your love and commitment to his well-being. He needs to know that you will be there for him and that he is a top priority, even though you have additional responsibilities that require your time. He needs to see concrete expressions of that love during the good times and the bad. In other words, a child needs to see that you love him just as much on his bad days as you do on his best.

Practical expressions of love should include the following:

- Verbal reassurance of *specific* things that you like about each child.
- Physical contact with your child, including hugs, kisses, back scratches, and so on. (I still remember my mom waking me up on school days by gently scratching my back.)
- Notes and cards that express pleasure with something your child has done or something you like about his personality. (This is particularly helpful for the noncustodial parent to do.)
- Spending individual time with each child. Find a hobby or activity that you can share with each child alone.
- Actively listening to your child. Focus on him and what he is saying. Stop what you are doing and give him good eye contact. Do not give advice or simplistic answers, but try to view the information through his eyes.
- (For the noncustodial parent) Frequent phone calls during the week, focusing on him and his day. Also, give him a number where you can be reached at almost any time. He needs to be assured that he has easy access to you when he feels he needs to talk about something.

No one is capable of displaying unconditional love at all times. However, if this is our goal, then we also need to be able to ask for forgiveness when we "lose it" with our kids. If you grew up in a home that was less than loving, then you may have particular difficulty expressing love to your children. For a more in-depth look at learning how to love your children, I recommend the following books: *How to Really Love Your Child* and *How to Really Love Your Teenager* by Ross Campbell (see appendix under Parenting).

Rebuild Trusting Relationships

One of the casualties of a divorce is the ability to trust again, at least in the immediate aftermath. This is just as true for children as it is for adults. As a parent, it is primarily *your* responsibility to rebuild your child's trust, because you are probably the most influential adult in his life. You may also be the target of his distrust if you were the one who left or if you are perceived as having betrayed the family in some way.

Rebuilding trust takes time and above all it requires your complete honesty. This is demonstrated in the way you explain divorce to your children, whether or not you "scapegoat" your own mistakes, how honest you are with your own feelings, and whether or not you keep your word to the children. In an effort to compensate the children for the losses experienced in the divorce, some parents compound the mistake by making promises to the children that they are not sure they can keep. The promised vacations, trips to Disney World, and extravagant toys do not tell the children that you love them. And if the promises aren't kept, this reinforces a belief that Mom or Dad can't be trusted.

Even if you got away with minor unfulfilled promises before the divorce, what you must realize after the divorce is that your life is under a microscope. Your children are testing to see if they can trust you again. Therefore you must take special care to measure your words before you speak.

These promises include the negative ones too. Have you ever told your children, "If I hear you whine one more time, I'll send you to your room for a month"? Don't say it unless you can follow through on your word! This may seem like a minor infraction of which we have all been guilty, but now more than ever it is imperative that you think before you speak.

Think about the following statements:

"If you do that one more time, I'll kill you!"
"If you don't clean up your plate, you won't eat for a week."
"If you don't get in the car right now, I'll never take you to Grandma's again."

Besides the fact that you shouldn't make such harsh statements, think about the message that these words convey to your children regarding your trustworthiness. I know that we've all sent these messages or not followed through on a commitment merely because it slipped our minds. When we become aware of these mistakes, it is important that we, once again, speak the truth as lovingly as we can: "I'm sorry I said that. Mommy didn't really mean that she wouldn't feed you for a week. I only said that out of frustration. You need to finish your meal or you won't get any dessert."

"I know Daddy said he would take you fishing this weekend, but I forgot that I had to get the car inspected. That was my fault for not remembering. I know that you're disappointed, but I'm sure we will be able to go some other time. How about if we do this instead . . . ?

Provide Firm, Loving Discipline

Another casualty in many divorcing families is a consistent level of loving discipline (assuming it was formerly present). As they lose touch with their children or lose the energy to keep up with their shenanigans, many parents take the easy way out, which is to give in or react in haste. Yet to the child of divorce, consistent discipline is key to his feeling secure and loved.

It is not within the scope of this book to cover the full range of discipline techniques; therefore I will review a few guidelines and then recommend some books.

Make the punishment fit the crime. This takes a great deal of wisdom and no one can be there to tell you how to handle each new situation. The bottom line is don't overreact to minor infractions, but take seriously the mistakes that carry long-term implications. The way this is played out in many homes is for parents to let things slide until they've had enough. Then they react with the back of their hand or a threat on which everyone knows they will not follow through.

Logical consequences make the most sense and also teach valuable lessons. Here are some examples:

"If you don't put away your toys, I'll have to take them away for a couple of days."

"If you don't turn off your Play Station now, you won't be allowed to play with it tomorrow."

"Since I don't like to see you act that way, go sit in the other room until you're done pouting."

Following through on the consequences to each situation requires thought and patience. This means that you need to stay calm and not react in the anger of the moment.

Your immediate reaction is usually not the best way to respond.

Pick your battles. Which matters are important enough to fight over? Particularly with teenagers, you could fight over just about anything. But since discipline takes a lot of thought and energy, you may decide not to battle over whether your son eats everything on his plate or whether your daughter can wear makeup to school. You need to decide in advance which issues are most important and on which matters you need to have some latitude.

Distinguish between accidents, disobedience, and defiance. Even though accidents may be devastating to you personally, you don't want to deal with them as harshly as you would with disobedience or defiance. For example, if my daughter spills her juice on my computer and ruins it, I'm going to be very upset (especially if I'm at the end of a chapter that I haven't yet saved to the disk). But it might be punishment enough for her to see how upset I am. In fact I'd probably end up hugging her and assuring her: "It's okay, I realize that it was an accident."

However, if I tell her to sit in the kitchen and drink her juice and instead she walks into my office and spills her juice, I need to punish her for disobedience. Sitting her in her chair for a while would be appropriate at younger ages, even though my anger at the moment may want me to do more.

The most serious infraction, however, would be defiance—if my daughter looked me right in the eye and poured the juice on my computer, right after I told her to take her juice back to the kitchen. For this, a young child could be spanked or restricted to her room. An older child might have to work in order to replace the computer that was ruined (logical consequence of her action).

As you can see from the example, the result of the child's behavior is the same. My computer is ruined. The difference that you need to distinguish before you discipline is this: Was it an accident, disobedience, or defiance?

Explain to your children the difference between your feelings toward them and your feelings about their behaviors. In other words, tell your children, "I love you but I don't like the way you are behaving."

Remember when your parents used to say, "This is going to hurt me more than it will hurt you" just before they spanked you? Even though that used to drive us crazy at the time, I believe those words carried a message of love.

Think about the following statements and how they could be rephrased in more loving ways:

"You're stupid" might become "I know you are very capable but the way you're acting right now isn't very smart."

"Shut up!" could be stated, "I want to listen to you, but could you please stop talking right now so that I can think?"

"I hate it when you do that!" could be modified to "I love you but I don't like it when you do that."

These changes seem obvious in the calm reality of the present, but they take great willpower and thought when you reach the height of your frustration. I guess that's why people say, "Parenting is hard work!"

Two books that take a closer look at issues of disciplining your children are *The New Dare to Discipline* by James Dobson and *Making Children Mind without Losing Yours* by Kevin Leman (see "Parenting" in the Recommended Reading section).

Foster Healthy Relationships

As a single parent, it is very important that you promote healthy role models for your children. This usually includes monitoring who they hang out with, finding positive opposite-sex and same-sex adult relationships, and providing some exposure to healthy, intact families. Here are a few guidelines to help you accomplish this.

Insist on meeting your children's friends. Even if they are teenagers, you are entitled to know whom your children are hanging around with and to guide their selection. Try to be friendly and open-minded toward all of them. Be very cautious about disapproving of any of their friends, since this can make the relationships even more important to your children. Remember, you can't always pick your children's friends. To even suggest a person as a potential friend can sometimes be the kiss of death for that relationship. Usually, the most you can do is put your children in places where they will be in contact with a desirable peer group (church, the YMCA, clubs, civic groups, and so on).

Find adult role models who will be stable and reliable influences for your children. This is especially important if your former mate does not provide that type of support. If the other parent is not very involved with your children, then a role model of the opposite sex is critical. This should be a family friend, a grandparent, an uncle or aunt—someone you can count on to be there for your kids over the long haul, *not* a series of boyfriends or girlfriends who may be in and out of your life.

If this role model is a friend, then it works best if the person is primarily interested in helping your children and not trying to get closer to you. If no one has shown a real interest in filling this role, you may want to ask a friend or relative specifically to help out in this way. They may not realize the need and may be flattered that you asked.

Even though many of your friendships will evolve away from married couples and toward singles, it is important that you maintain relationships with some happily married couples. It is good for both you and your children to observe some happily married couples, so that you don't lose your perspective. One teenager recently told me, "I don't know if I'll ever get married. I don't know of a single family where there hasn't been a divorce or of one that isn't headed in that direction." Another girl told me, "I'm real nervous around men. I've never lived in a home with a man because my dad left when I was three. Whenever I'm around couples, I always check out the husband and wife to see how they act. I want to know what a normal family looks like for when I get married. That is, if that ever happens." Spending time with relatives and friends who are married, both during holidays and when they're just doing their daily routine, can be a very important part of your child's development.

Build a Positive Sense of Self-Worth

No matter what job you have, your most important responsibility is raising your children. And probably one of the greatest gifts that you can pass on to your children is a balanced self-image. Of all the problems that I see in counseling and in day-to-day contact with people, the most prevalent and pervasive is that of insecurity and poor self-image. To some extent, we *all* struggle with this from time to time.

Each of us must ask, What does our society value in a person, and what values do I reinforce in my home?

Unfortunately, in most settings, children see that they are valued primarily in four areas: beauty, brains, brawn, and bucks. Our society reflects these values in everything from advertising and cartoons to election results in the local school board or women's club.

If children are not good-looking or smart, they often feel like failures and may be treated that way by classmates. This is particularly true for girls, who often feel special pressure to look like Barbie dolls or at least like the latest young pop star. Boys on the other hand can get away with not being exceptionally handsome or smart, as long as they are strong or good at sports.

The fourth area of value is one that we adults know well. Yet you may be surprised at how important money is to a child's popularity and standing with his peers. Our children must wear the right clothes, have the latest games and toys, and even have the correct label on their sneakers. Children are also keenly aware of who lives in the right neighborhoods and whose parents are influential in the community.

If a child does not have at least one of the four ingredients—beauty, brains, brawn, or bucks—then it will be an uphill struggle for that child to achieve acceptance in our society. One difficult truth that complicates this problem is that, no matter how blessed we may be, there is always someone out there who is a little prettier, smarter, stronger, or richer. And no matter how many of the ingredients of success we have, we will still struggle from time to time with a negative self-image.

Given these difficulties, how can you help to develop a positive self-image in your child? Let me briefly describe some general guidelines and then recommend a few books that expand on this topic.

First and foremost, you need to love yourself before you can properly love others. If you do not have a good self-image, then your first task is to get help for yourself so that you can model a positive self-image to your children.

You need to counterbalance what their peer group values. When your children are with you, you need to show them a secure kind of love—one that is not based on how they look or act, but one that values and loves them all the time. As mentioned earlier, you need to show them a love that is unconditional.

Nurture your children with physical attention and concrete expressions of love. Hug your children, touch them often, be sure to mention regularly specific things that you like about each child.

Encourage your children to be open and honest with their feelings. Don't negate their feelings even when you disagree with them. For example, "I'm sorry you feel like you're not loved. I can understand how much that hurts. But let me assure you that you are loved." You need to provide an example of open and honest communication.

Foster independence in your children. Remember, your goal is not to create obedient clones but responsible adults. Therefore you must encourage your children's decision making and willingness to try things on their own, even when you think it may lead to failure. When they do fail, allow them to suffer the consequences, but then be there for them emotionally, encouraging them to try again.

Some additional guidelines can be found in the following books: *How to Really Love Your Child* and *How to Really Love Your Teenager* by Ross Campbell and *Raising Positive Kids in a Negative World* by Zig Ziglar (see "Parenting" in the Recommended Reading section).

Give a Sense of Purpose

The ability to give children a sense of purpose and meaning in their lives is a parenting skill that is usually overlooked, and yet it's critically important for your child's healthy development. Children and adults *need* to have something in their lives that gives them meaning and purpose. For some it is their work, for others it may be in serving their fellow man, while others seek a personal relationship with God. Whatever your pursuit, you have probably come to find that living solely for yourself and your needs is an unfulfilling, selfish quest. Instead, many have found greater fulfillment when they live their lives for something or someone beyond themselves.

One of the failures of the Yuppie generation was in their pursuit of wealth and power, devoid of ethical considerations. In Ecclesiastes King Solomon, one of the richest and most powerful men of his time, said that all the world has to offer is a vain pursuit. As we teach our children how to make their way in this world, we must not forget that a faith or belief system should be part of the fabric of our lives.

I hear many parents almost apologize for what they believe. This sends a message to our children about how important our moral values are to us. I realize that many don't want to offend others, but with our children, we have an obligation to present a firm set of values that tell us who we are and why we are here. Young children will not understand these concepts, and your teenagers will rebel against them, so many parents ask, "Why bother?" The answer is one that you have heard before. Children may not understand it now or may not want to hear it later, but the seeds you plant today will have a big influence on how they live as adults. Solomon puts it this way in the Book of Proverbs:

"Train up a child in the way he should go, and when he is old, he will not depart from it" (Prov. 22:6).

There are many things that you will want to teach your children as they grow up, but I believe the best way to teach a belief system is to live it. You obviously don't want to preach it without practicing it. That would only create an opposite reaction. If you don't have meaning or purpose in your own life, then obviously that needs to be settled first and foremost (see appendix under Spiritual Life).

Key to Accepting Your Circumstances

Let's shift our focus from our children to ourselves. Actually, we have come full circle in this book. In the first chapter, I mentioned the Serenity Prayer, and how important it can be to have an attitude of acceptance toward the things that you cannot change. I then went on to discuss the things that you can change and how you can effect positive change in your children. Now, in this final section, we will take a closer look at how your attitude toward your circumstances can affect your entire life.

The parents' attitude about their situation has a large bearing on how they interact with their former spouse, how they relate with their children, and the speed at which their own recovery takes place. Let's contrast two situations.

Both Mrs. A and Mrs. B are suburban housewives. As these women were approaching their fortieth birthdays, their husbands left them for younger women. Both women were devastated by the loss, as were their children. Neither woman was educated beyond high school and neither has worked since getting married.

Mrs. A views herself as a victim. She is angry with her ex-spouse and boasts about giving him a hard time. She got full legal and physical custody of their three children, along with four years of alimony, so that she could be trained for some type of new career. Presently, about two years after her divorce, Mrs. A is working as a receptionist for little more than minimum wage. She has no plans for her vocational education because she says she's really not very good at anything. "Besides," she explained, "I never wanted this divorce in the first place. I don't think I should have to work when I have three kids at home."

Mrs. A has very few social outlets, and many of her married friends are now drifting away from her. She is feeling more and more isolated and tells her children about how unfair all of this has been for her. Her children feel sorry for her and feel guilty when they want to visit their dad. He has been sporadic in his visits and late with many of his payments, but as he puts it, "At least I'm still there for them when they need me."

Mrs. B, on the other hand, seems to be doing well. After her divorce, she went back to school and now, two years later, is well along in her business administration degree. She has already started her own small business, doing word processing out of her home. She has physical custody of her two children, but she and her ex-husband have joint legal custody. Mrs. B requested this arrangement because she knew that her husband would stay more involved in the kids' lives if he had some continuing input into their upbringing. As she put it, "I may not be married to him, but he is still their father. Even though he didn't turn out to be such a good husband, he was always a good father, and I believe he still is."

Mr. B feels very connected with his children, and they enjoy their visits with him. They feel good about leaving for his place and good about telling Mom all about their weekends, because they know that their mother encourages the relationship.

Mrs. B is also very involved socially. She has found a whole new support system, with friends who have been through similar life changes. Yet she still stays friendly with one or two of the married couples with whom she was formerly connected. Mrs. B has described her life in this way: "I wouldn't wish divorce on my worst enemy, but I wouldn't trade anything for what I have learned after having gone through a divorce. I have more self-confidence and feel more fulfilled now than I ever have. While I was married, I never would have thought I could make it on my own, but now I know I can. I understand more about myself and other people, which I think has made me a better friend to my friends, a better parent to my kids, and a better overall person. Sure I get lonely sometimes, but there are worse things than being single and lonely, and one of them is to be in a bad marriage. Besides, now I have much stronger friendships, with people I know I can count on when I need a listening ear."

In our Fresh Start seminars we describe a poster that features a man with a funnel in his head, and a spigot where his nose should be. In the funnel is a bunch of lemons and out of the spigot lemonade is pouring into a pitcher. The caption reads, "When life gives you lemons, make lemonade."

This is a perfect illustration of how divorce affects our lives. We have all been given some lemons in our lives. (Some of us married them.) Yet, in spite of these bitter experiences, we still have the ability to choose our own attitude toward our circumstances. Will we choose to become bitter, to squeeze those lemons and serve other people lemon juice? You know what happens when someone serves lemon juice. The sour taste turns people away. We alienate our friends, our children, and ourselves.

Or will we choose to add some sugar to that lemon juice and serve lemonade? The sugar that we all possess is our own sweet disposition—the ability to forgive, to love, and to uplift others. When we add this to the bitter experiences of life, we find a perfect combination of sweet and sour that attracts others, like lemonade on a hot day.

Charles Swindoll, in his book *Strengthening Your Grip* (see "Spiritual Life" in the Recommended Reading section), explains this concept:

> The colorful, nineteenth-century showman and gifted violinist Nicolo Paganini was standing before a packed house, playing through a difficult piece of music. A full orchestra surrounded him with magnificent support. Suddenly one string on his violin snapped and hung gloriously down from his instrument. Beads of perspiration popped out on his forehead. He frowned but continued to play, improvising beautifully.
>
> To the conductor's surprise, a second string broke. And shortly thereafter, a third. Now there were three limp strings dangling from Paganini's violin as the master performer completed the difficult composition on the one remaining string. The audience jumped to its feet and in good Italian fashion, filled the hall with shouts and screams, "Bravo! Bravo!" As the applause died down, the violinist asked the people to sit back down. Even though they knew there was no way they could expect an encore, they quietly sank back into their seats.
>
> He held the violin high for everyone to see. He nodded at the conductor to begin the encore and then he turned back to the crowd, and with a twinkle in his eye, he smiled and shouted, "Paganini . . . and one string!" After that he placed the single-stringed Stradivarius

beneath his chin and played the final piece on *one* string as the audience (and the conductor) shook their heads in silent amazement. "Paganini . . . and one string!" *And,* I might add, an attitude of fortitude.

Dr. Victor Frankl, the bold, courageous Jew who became a prisoner during the Holocaust, endured years of indignity and humiliation by the Nazis before he was finally liberated. At the beginning of his ordeal, he marched into a Gestapo courtroom. His captors had taken away his home and family, his cherished freedom, his possessions, even his watch and wedding ring. They had shaved his head and stripped his clothing off his body. There he stood before the German high command, under the glaring lights being interrogated and falsely accused. He was destitute, a helpless pawn in the hands of brutal, prejudiced, sadistic men. He had nothing. No, that isn't true. He suddenly realized there was one thing no one could ever take away from him—just one. Do you know what it was?

Dr. Frankl realized he still had the power to choose his own attitude. No matter what anyone would ever do to him, regardless of what the future held for him, the attitude choice was his to make. Bitterness or forgiveness. To give up or to go on. Hatred or hope. Determination to endure or the paralysis of self-pity. It boiled down to "Frankl . . . and one string."

Words can never adequately convey the incredible impact of our attitude toward life. The longer I live, the more convinced I become that life is 10 percent what happens to us and 90 percent how we respond to it (pp. 205–6).

For you, the question remains, What will *your* attitude be toward *your* circumstances? Will it be bitterness, self-pity, and immobilization, as with Mrs. A? Or will you choose forgiveness, hope, endurance, and determination, as Mrs. B described? What kind of music are you going to play on that one string of yours?

Now I know you're thinking, "Yeah, but you don't understand how much I've been hurt." Or, "You can't imagine what a creep I was married to." Look again at the life of Victor Frankl. You could not have suffered as much as he. *Are you going to be a victim or a victor?* And before you answer that you'd rather remain in your self-pity, think about your children. Do you want *them* to overcome their circumstances? And what attitude would you like for them to choose? The research has demonstrated that the attitude of the parent, and especially the custodial parent, is the biggest predictor of the child's adjustment.

Even though you have had some terrible things happen to you as a family, I believe there is still great hope. You *can* serve lemonade, and your children can serve lemonade too. You and they don't need to be victims. It's your choice. Despite the challenges, there is great hope for children of divorce.

Summary

Some of the most important keys for parenting, especially as single parents, are:

1. Provide a loving environment for your child.
2. Rebuild trusting relationships.
3. Provide firm, loving discipline.
4. Foster healthy relationships.
5. Build a positive sense of self-worth.
6. Give your children a sense of purpose and meaning in their lives.

Your attitude has a lot to do with how well you accomplish these goals. Your attitude toward your situation affects your recovery and that of your children. I believe that your decision to play beautiful music on whatever strings you have left is the most important gift that you can pass on to your children.

Recommended Reading

The following books are recommended readings available from Fresh Start Seminars. Each deals with specific issues surrounding divorce and single parenting. Most of these books are available through booksellers or can be ordered by calling our office at 1–800–882–2799 during regular business hours (E.S.T.). Please have your VISA or MasterCard ready if you would like to order by phone. Written requests should be sent to Fresh Start Seminars, Attn: Tom, 1440 Russell Rd., Paoli, PA 19301. Or, write to us at *whitemant@aol.com*. Make your checks payable to Fresh Start. Discounts are available for orders of more than ten books. Prices are approximate and subject to change.

Anger

Carter, Les, and Frank Minirth. *The Anger Workbook*. Nashville: Thomas Nelson, 1996, $16.

Learner, Harriet. *Dance of Anger*. New York: Harper Perennial, 1985, $14.

Children's Books

Sprague, Gary. *Kids Hope for Children* (Grades 1–5). Elgin, Ill.: David C. Cook, 1997, $14.

———. *Kids Hope for Teens* (Grades 6–12). Elgin, Ill.: David C. Cook, 1997, $14.

Depression

Burns, David, M.D. *The Feeling Good Handbook*. New York: Plume Printing, 1999, $18.

Emery, Gary. *Getting Undepressed*. New York: Simon & Schuster, 1988, $12.

Greenberger, Dennis, and Christine Padesky. *Mind over Mood*. New York: Guilford Press, 1995, $21.

Divorce Recovery

Burns, Bob, and Thomas Whiteman. *The Fresh Start Divorce Recovery Workbook*. Nashville: Thomas Nelson, 1998, $16.

Carder, Dave. *Torn Asunder: Recovering from Extramarital Affairs*. Chicago: Moody Press, 1992, $15.

Whiteman, Thomas, and Randy Petersen. *Starting Over*. Colorado Springs: Piñon Press, 2001, $15.

Parenting

Berry, Richard L. *Angry Kids: Understanding and Managing the Emotions That Control Them*. Grand Rapids: Revell, 2001, $17.

Campbell, Ross. *How to Really Love Your Child.* Wheaton, Ill.: Chariot Victor Books, 1992, $10.

———. *How to Really Love Your Teenager.* Wheaton, Ill.: Chariot Victor Books, 1993, $10.

Cloud, Henry, and John Townsend. *Boundaries with Kids.* Grand Rapids: Zondervan, 1998, $20.

Dobson, James. *The New Dare to Discipline.* Wheaton, Ill.: Tyndale House, 1996, $13.

Faber, Adele, and Elaine Mazlish. *How to Talk So Kids Will Listen and Listen So Kids Will Talk.* New York: Avon Books, 1999, $13.

Gordon, Jeenie. *Those Turbulent Teen Years,* 2d ed. Grand Rapids: Revell, 2000, $6.

Gordon, Dr. Thomas. *Parent Effectiveness Training: The Proven Program for Raising Responsible Children.* New York: Three Rivers Press, 2000, $15.

Leman, Dr. Kevin. *Making Children Mind without Losing Yours.* Grand Rapids: Revell, 2000, $14.

Whiteman, Thomas. *A Fresh Start for Single Parents.* Colorado Springs: David C. Cook, 1997, $16.

Ziglar, Zig. *Raising Positive Kids in a Negative World.* New York: Ballantine Books, 1996, $12.

Relationships

Cloud, Henry, and John Townsend. *Boundaries.* Grand Rapids: Zondervan, 1992, $20.

———. *Safe People.* Grand Rapids: Zondervan, 1996, $13.

Jones, Tom. *Sex and Love When You're Single Again.* Nashville: Thomas Nelson, 1990, $9.

———. *The Single Again Handbook.* Nashville: Thomas Nelson, 1993, $12.

Whiteman, Thomas, and Randy Petersen. *Victim of Love?* Colorado Springs: Piñon Press, 1998, $13.

Remarriage

Burns, Cherie. *Stepmotherhood: How to Survive without Feeling Frustrated, Left Out, or Wicked.* New York: Three Rivers Press, 2001, $12.

Cloud, Henry, and John Townsend. *Boundaries in Marriage.* Grand Rapids: Zondervan, 1999, $20.

Frydenger, Tom, and Adrienne Frydenger. *The Blended Family,* Grand Rapids: Revell, 1985, $10.

Wright, H. Norman. *Before You Remarry.* Eugene, Ore.: Harvest House, 1999, $10.

Self-Esteem

Dobson, James. *The New Hide or Seek: Building Self-Esteem in Your Child.* Grand Rapids: Revell, 1999, $14.

McGee, Robert. *The Search for Significance.* Dallas: Word, 1998, $12.

Whiteman, Thomas, and Randy Petersen. *Be Your Own Best Friend.* Grand Rapids: Revell, 2001, $6.

Separation

Chapman, Gary. *Hope for the Separated.* Chicago: Moody Press, 1996, $12.

Whiteman, Thomas, and Thomas Bartlett. *Marriage Mender.* Colorado Springs: NavPress, 1996, $12.

Special Needs

Barkley, Russell. *Taking Charge of ADHD: The Complete Authoritative Guide for Parents.* New York: Guilford Press, 2000, $19.

Cook, Rosemarie. *Parenting a Child with Special Needs.* Grand Rapids: Zondervan, 1992, $10.

Ferber, Richard, M.D. *Solving Your Child's Sleep Problems.* New York: Fireside Book, 1985, $13.

Spiritual Life

Lewis, C. S. *Mere Christianity.* New York: Touchstone Books, 1996, $8.

Lucado, Max. *Lucado 3 in 1.* Nashville: Thomas Nelson, 2000, $17. (These are three great devotionals and anything by Max Lucado is highly recommended.)

Swindoll, Charles. *Strengthening Your Grip.* Dallas: Word, 1998, $16.

Yancey, Philip. *Disappointment with God.* Grand Rapids: Zondervan, 1997, $6.

Thomas Whiteman, with a Ph.D. in psychology and human development, is the founder and president of Life Counseling Services and the Mid-Atlantic director of Fresh Start Seminars. He conducts more than fifty divorce recovery seminars a year throughout the United States. Dr. Whiteman directs one of the largest outpatient practices in the country, employing more than one hundred therapists. He is a frequent speaker at seminars and workshops and is an adjunct professor at Eastern College. Dr. Whiteman is the author or co-author of fourteen books. He and his wife, Lori, have three children and live in Berwyn, Pennsylvania.